Counselling
Survivors of
Childhood
Sexual Abuse

Counselling in Practice

Series editor: Windy Dryden
Associate editor: E. Thomas Dowd

Counselling in Practice is a series of books developed especially for counsellors and students of counselling which provides practical, accessible guidelines for dealing with specific, but very common problems. Books in this series have become recognized as classic texts in their field and SAGE is pleased to announce second editions of the following:

Counselling for Depression
Paul Gilbert

Counselling Survivors of Childhood Sexual Abuse
Claire Burke Draucker

New in the series:

Counselling for Eating Disorders
Sara Gilbert

Counselling
Survivors of
Childhood
Sexual Abuse

Second Edition

Claire Burke Draucker

SAGE Publications
London • Thousand Oaks • New Delhi

First edition published as *Counselling Survivors of Childhood Sexual Abuse* 1992
Reprinted in 1993, 1994, 1996, 1998
This edition first published 2000

 SAGE Publications Ltd
6 Bonhill Street
London EC2A 4PU

SAGE Publications Inc
2455 Teller Road
Thousand Oaks, California 91320

SAGE Publications India Pvt Ltd
32, M-Block Market
Greater Kailash – I
New Delhi 110 048

British Library Cataloguing in Publication data

A catalogue record for this book is available from the British Library

ISBN 0 7619 6580 7
ISBN 0 7619 6581 5 (pbk)

Library of Congress catalog record available

Typeset by Mayhew Typesetting, Rhayader, Powys
Printed in Great Britain by Biddles Ltd, Guildford, Surrey

Contents

1

Introduction

C hildhood sexual abuse is often a significant trauma that may have a lifelong impact on survivors. When adult survivors of childhood sexual abuse seek counselling for any reason, counsellors must be prepared to explore with them the role the abuse has played in their development and the effect it might be having on their present concerns. Due to the prevalence of childhood sexual abuse in the histories of individuals who seek counselling, and its possible pervasive and long-term effects, it is important that all counsellors become adept at addressing the unique and complex needs of survivors.

This chapter will address several basic issues related to the phenomenon of childhood sexual abuse. Topics include the definition of childhood sexual abuse, the recognition of sexual abuse as a significant social problem, and empirical research findings related to adult survivors. In addition, several fundamental counselling issues are addressed and the structure of the book is outlined.

Definition of childhood sexual abuse

Defining childhood sexual abuse has been problematic for both researchers and clinicians. Definitions in the literature vary according to the types of activities considered to be 'sexual' and the circumstances considered to constitute abuse. Finkelhor (1997) suggested that the following definition, formulated by the National Center on Child Abuse and Neglect (NCCAN, 1978: 2), is consistent with most legal and research definitions of child sexual abuse:

> Contacts or interactions between a child and an adult when the child is being used for the sexual stimulation of the perpetrator or another person. Sexual abuse may also be committed by a person under the age of 18 when that person is significantly older than the victim or when the perpetrator is in a position of power or control over another child.

Finkelhor argued that this definition has several essential components. It includes both intra-familial and extra-familial abuse, as well as contact and non-contact activities. The definition also emphasizes the exploitation of adult authority and addresses the maturation advantage of the perpetrator over the child. Because this broad definition has important clinical relevance, it is appropriate for a book that focuses on childhood sexual abuse as a counselling concern.

The recognition of sexual abuse as a significant social problem

The phenomenon of child sexual abuse was historically denied by the public and by mental health professionals. Herman (1981) outlined three 'discoveries' of the prevalence of sexual abuse in our society. The awareness of the occurrence of sexual abuse as a traumatic experience in the lives of children is usually traced to Freud, who is credited with the first 'discovery' of incest. When female patients in large numbers revealed to Freud that they had childhood sexual experiences with adult men in their families, Freud initially suggested that these traumatic experiences were the cause of hysteria; this became known as the seduction theory. In the service of protecting the patriarchal family structure, Freud identified the perpetrators of the sexual abuse as other children, caretakers, or more distant relatives – but not fathers. In response to peer pressure, however, Freud eventually repudiated the seduction theory and claimed instead that his patients' frequent reports of sexual abuse were incestuous fantasies rather than actual childhood events.

Herman (1981: 10) reported that for decades following Freud's repudiation of the seduction theory, professionals maintained a 'dignified silence' on the topic of incest and the public continued to deny the reality and the prevalence of childhood sexual abuse. It was not until the 1940s that incest was 'discovered' for a second time by social scientists conducting large-scale survey studies of sexual practices, including the now famous Kinsey study (Kinsey et al., 1953). These studies documented that between 20 and 30 per cent of the women who responded to the surveys reported having had a sexual experience as a child with a male, between 4 and 12 per cent reported a sexual experience with a relative, and 1 per cent reported a sexual experience with a father or stepfather. Although the sexual abuse of boys was not addressed in several of these studies, one researcher (Landis, 1956) reported that 30 per cent of the male participants in his survey reported a childhood sexual experience with an adult, who was most typically a male.

Despite the substantiation of childhood sexual abuse provided by these studies, the reality of the phenomenon continued to be denied. For example, most of the sexually abused women in the Kinsey study reported being disturbed by the experience. The researchers indicated, however, that the women's distress resulted from social conditioning rather than the sexual act itself. Herman concluded that Kinsey and his colleagues, in their attempt to encourage enlightenment and tolerance of sexual attitudes, 'failed to distinguish between essentially harmless acts committed by consenting adults, "nuisance acts" such as exhibitionism, and frankly exploitative acts such as the prostitution of women and the molesting of children' (1981: 17).

Herman (1981) dated the 'third discovery' of incest to the 1970s, and credited the feminist movement with bringing the problem of childhood sexual abuse into public awareness, along with other taboo issues such as wife battering and rape. This was followed by legitimate, scientific studies of the problem and public revelations of incest survivors who chose to tell their stories.

Empirical research related to childhood sexual abuse

Research related to childhood sexual abuse has focused primarily on determining its prevalence in the population and in clinical subgroups, identifying long-term effects that stem from the abuse, relating specific abuse characteristics to long-term effects, and exploring what factors might mediate the relationship between abuse characteristics and adult functioning. This research will be briefly reviewed and summarized.

Prevalence

Researchers now generally agree that the occurrence of childhood sexual abuse is much more frequent than originally believed. Studies have reported, however, a wide variation in prevalence rates – that is, the proportion of the population that has experienced childhood sexual abuse. Wurtele and Miller-Perrin (1992) reviewed several large-scale studies involving college and community samples and found that the prevalence rates of childhood sexual abuse ranged from 7 per cent to 62 per cent for women and 3 per cent to 16 per cent for men. In clinical and forensic samples, these rates are often much higher (Gordon and Alexander, 1993). Prevalence rates are affected by the way sexual abuse is operationally defined (e.g. the types of sexual activities included), the characteristics of the sample studied (e.g. college samples versus random national samples), and variations in research methodology (e.g. face-to-face interviews versus surveys).

In a national US telephone survey of 2,626 adults, 27 per cent of the women and 16 per cent of the men reported having experienced sexual abuse involving physical contact during their childhood (Finkelhor et al., 1990). The Third National Incidence Study on Child Abuse and Neglect (NIS–3) (US Department of Health and Human Services, 1996) indicated that in 1993, 217,700 children were moderately or severely harmed as a result of sexual abuse. Finkelhor (1994) reviewed 21 international population studies of child sexual abuse, primarily from English-speaking and northern European countries. The prevalence rates of child sexual abuse in these studies ranged from 7 per cent to 36 per cent for women and from 3 per cent to 29 per cent for men. Despite the differences in numbers, research suggests that a significant portion of adults have experienced some form of sexual abuse as children.

Long-term effects

Just as the prevalence of childhood sexual abuse was denied, the long-term effects of sexual abuse have historically been minimized. Some have maintained that sexual activity between a child and an adult is harmless. Ramsey (1979), for example, suggested that incest could have beneficial results if it were not for society's negative reactions to it. Research has revealed, however, that a history of child sexual abuse is associated with numerous and varied long-term psychological, behavioural, interpersonal, and physical effects.

Psychological effects of childhood sexual trauma have been identified in several comprehensive reviews of research on the long-term consequences of child sexual abuse (Beitchman et al., 1992; Browne and Finkelhor, 1986; Finkelhor, 1990; Polusny and Follette, 1995). Studies have shown that child sexual abuse is associated with an increased level of general psychological distress, depression, anxiety (phobias, panic disorder, obsessive symptoms) and long-term post-traumatic effects (Bifulco et al., 1991; Fromuth and Burkhart, 1989; Pribor and Dinwiddie, 1992; Roland et al., 1989; Saunders et al., 1992; Stein et al., 1988).

Associations between a history of child sexual abuse and behavioural or relationship effects that may pose health risks have been documented. Women who were sexually abused as children are more likely to report a lifetime prevalence of alcohol abuse/ dependence and drug abuse/dependence than women who were not abused (Stein et al., 1988). Certain types of eating disorders, including obesity, have been associated with child sexual abuse (Bushnell et al., 1992; Calam and Slade, 1987, 1989; Smolak et al., 1990; Springs and Friedrich, 1992). A sexual abuse history is relatively rare in restrictive anorexia, more common in anorexia of the bulimic subtype, and most common in bulimia without a history of anorexia (Waller, 1991, 1992a, 1992b).

Women with a history of child sexual abuse also report more adult sexual behaviours associated with health risk, including an earlier age at first intercourse, a greater number of sexual partners, and a higher rate of unintended and aborted pregnancies (Springs and Friedrich, 1992; Stein et al., 1988; Wyatt et al., 1992; Zierler et al., 1991). One study demonstrated that when sexual abuse is accompanied by other forms of abuse (e.g. physical abuse), it may be associated with HIV-risk behaviours, such as not using condoms, engaging in prostitution, and using injectable drugs (Cunningham et al., 1994). Accumulated data from numerous studies suggest a significant relationship between childhood sexual abuse and experiences of victimization in adulthood, including adult sexual assault and partner physical violence (Chu and Dill, 1990; Elliot and Briere, 1993; Walker et al., 1993; Wyatt et al., 1992).

A history of child sexual abuse has been associated with a number of medical problems in adult women (Laws, 1993). While research findings implicating child sexual abuse in the development of specific diseases have been equivocal, associations between a history of sexual abuse and self-report of a variety of medical problems and concerns have been reported (Friedman and Schnurr, 1995; Fry, 1993). For example, there is a high prevalence of child sexual abuse histories in women who report chronic pelvic pain, backaches, headaches, and functional gastrointestinal disorders (Drossman et al., 1990; Felitti, 1991; Harrop-Griffiths et al., 1988; McCauley et al., 1997; Pecukonis, 1996; Reiter and Gambone, 1990; Reiter et al., 1991; Walker et al., 1988; Walker et al., 1992). Compared with women who were not abused, women who were sexually abused as children have reported more hospitalizations for illness, a greater number of physical and psychological problems, and lower ratings of overall health (Moeller et al., 1993); more medical problems and somatization (Springs and Friedrich, 1992); and poorer health perceptions, more functional limitations, more chronic disease, and a greater number of somatic symptoms (Golding, 1994).

Abuse situation characteristics

Researchers have attempted to determine whether certain characteristics of the sexual abuse situation or the aftermath are associated with long-term outcomes. Although the relationship between some characteristics (age at onset, duration) and severity of negative effects is unclear, sexual abuse that includes threats, force, or violence; involvement of a father or father figure; or invasive sexual activities (genital contact, vaginal or anal intercourse) seems to be particularly noxious (Beitchman et al., 1992; Browne and Finkelhor, 1986; Finkelhor, 1997). Negative reactions of significant others are associated with poorer outcomes; supportive responses have been shown to mitigate negative effects (Finkelhor, 1997).

Child sexual abuse and other forms of maltreatment

Childhood sexual abuse is often accompanied by other forms of childhood maltreatment. For example, psychological abuse (acts that are rejecting, isolating, terrorizing, ignoring, and corrupting) and physical abuse (hitting, kicking, punching, beating, and threatening or using a weapon) often accompany child sexual abuse (Briere, 1992; Garbarino et al., 1986). Also, child sexual abuse typically occurs in the context of general family dysfunction. Women who were sexually abused are more likely to report that their families of origin were emotionally distant (lacking in cohesiveness, devoid of intimacy), rigid (controlling, governed by rules and traditional roles, exhibiting low adaptability), and conflicted than are women who were not abused (Carson et al., 1990; Edwards and Alexander, 1992; Jackson et al., 1990; Yama et al., 1993). Because these differences tend to appear whether the abuse occurred within or outside of the family, it appears that even when a family member does not perpetrate the abuse, there may be an association between its occurrence and certain family interactional patterns (Yama et al., 1993).

Researchers who have investigated several types of childhood abuse (psychological, physical, and sexual), family-of-origin characteristics, and later outcomes report a complex relationship between childhood maltreatment and adult functioning. In some studies, researchers have found that sexual abuse experiences were related to later negative effects even when variables of general family functioning were controlled by various statistical procedures (Briere and Elliot, 1993; Greenwald et al., 1990). Other researchers have found that the relationships between experiences of sexual abuse and adult outcomes are mostly non-significant when family variables are controlled (Nash et al., 1993; Parker and Parker, 1991; Yama et al., 1992). Several studies have found that physical, psychological, and sexual abuse are associated with specific long-term effects beyond the effects they have in common

(Briere and Runtz, 1990; Hall et al., 1993; Wind and Silvern, 1992). In a study of college women, for example, a history of psychological abuse was specifically related to low self-esteem; physical abuse was specifically related to aggression toward others; and sexual abuse was specifically related to maladaptive sexual behaviour (Briere and Runtz, 1990). Cumulative evidence from a review of all the studies suggests that (a) family-of-origin dynamics and all forms of maltreatment are important in understanding adult outcomes, (b) the severity of the abuse and the presence of two or more types of abuse play a role in producing adult vulnerability to disturbance, and (c) sexual abuse experiences contribute to specific symptomatology in adulthood (Draucker, 1996).

Mediating factors

A few studies have begun to examine factors that might mediate the effects of abuse on long-term adjustment. Survivors who attribute negative events to internal, global, and stable factors (depressive attributions), are unable to find meaning in their abusive experiences or to regain a sense of mastery, or continue to blame themselves for the abuse, show poorer adjustment (Draucker, 1989, 1995; Gold, 1986; Silver et al., 1983; Wyatt and Newcomb, 1990). This line of research suggests that there are certain cognitive processes that might reduce the harmful effects of childhood sexual abuse.

Summary

Principles of counselling adult survivors are, therefore, based on research which suggests that childhood sexual abuse is prevalent in the population and in the histories of those who seek counselling, and that it often results in varied long-term effects. While certain characteristics of the abuse situation are related to long-term effects, these relationships can be mediated by certain psychological processes employed by survivors. As Herman (1981: 7) stated, 'To be sexually exploited by a known and trusted adult is a central and formative experience in the lives of countless women'. It is now also believed that the same could be said about the lives of countless men (Urquiza and Keating, 1990).

Theories of abuse effects

Several theories have been proposed to explain the relationship between childhood sexual abuse and negative outcomes in adulthood. Two theories that have been widely discussed and a framework that deals with the long-term effects of male survivors are presented here.

Disguised presentation of undisclosed incest

Gelinas was one of the first experts to organize the varied and commonly reported symptoms of incest survivors into a 'coherent, explanatory, and heuristic framework' (1983: 312). She identified three underlying negative effects: chronic, traumatic neurosis; continued relational imbalances; and increased intergenerational risk of incest.

The intense affect and vivid memories experienced by survivors following disclosure and discussion of the incest are referred to as *chronic traumatic neurosis*. Phases of denial or repression alternate with intrusive experiences of trauma repetition (e.g. nightmares, pseudo-hallucinations, obsessions, emotional repetitions, behavioural re-enactments). Symptoms such as depression, anxiety, and substance abuse are secondary elaborations related to the hidden and untreated traumatic neurosis.

The relational imbalances exhibited by survivors are considered to be a result of the family dynamics that produced and maintained the secret of the incest. Gelinas (1983) discussed a scenario that typifies the development of incestuous family dynamics. Parentification occurs when a child, often an eldest daughter, assumes responsibility for parental functions. The child learns to protect and nurture her parents, thereby developing a caretaking identity. She becomes skilful in meeting the needs of others, but denies her own needs. She chooses as a partner a man who requires caretaking, typically one who is needy, narcissistic, or insecure. As she might still be meeting the needs of her family of origin, she soon becomes emotionally depleted. When she and her husband have children, maternal caretaking is added to her responsibilities. She is then less able to attend to her husband's needs and might attempt to enlist his support. He feels both threatened and abandoned and becomes increasingly unavailable to her. She might then attempt to get emotional support from her child, often her eldest daughter, and this daughter then begins to experience parentification. The husband, if unable to meet his needs outside the family, may do so through his daughter. Sexual abuse is most likely to occur if the father is narcissistic, exhibits poor impulse control, and uses alcohol.

The daughter, now an incest survivor, becomes an adult who is also very skilful at caretaking, but who has a poor self-concept and lacks the social skills needed to meet her own needs (e.g. assertiveness). She is unable to establish mutually supportive relationships with others and becomes isolated or abused and exploited in the relationships she does establish. As she also remains emotionally depleted, she will experience parenting difficulties and another generation of parentification may begin.

The intergenerational risk of incest is due to the establishment of the relational imbalances discussed above. The incest survivor's daughter becomes at risk for incest as the processes of parentification and marital estrangement are repeated. The survivor, experiencing an untreated traumatic neurosis, will avoid stimuli that provoke memories of her own abuse and is therefore less likely to detect or attend to the sexual abuse of her daughter. Gelinas (1983) stressed that this does not suggest that the mother is to blame for the incest. Although each parent is responsible for the incestuous family dynamics, the offender alone is responsible for the sexual contact.

The profile of an incest survivor thus often includes a presenting problem of chronic depression with complications that stem from the affective disorder (e.g. substance abuse, suicidality), atypical dissociative elements (e.g. nightmares, depersonalization), impulsive behaviours (e.g. impulsive eating, drinking, spending; child abuse), and a history of parentification (e.g. premature responsibilities in childhood).

A self-trauma model

More recently, Briere (1996) posited a theoretical model of symptom development for adults severely abused as children. Briere suggested that three self-functions and capacities are affected by childhood abuse and neglect, accounting for the myriad difficulties exhibited by survivors later in life. These functions are identity (a consistent sense of personal existence), boundary (an awareness of the demarcation between self and others), and affect regulation, which consists of both affect modulation (the ability to engage in internal activities to reduce negative affect states) and affect tolerance (the ability to maintain negative affect without resorting to avoiding, soothing, or distracting external activities). Childhood maltreatment interferes with the development of those skills by disrupting parent–child attachment and psychosocial learning. The child's development of a sense of self-efficacy, social skills, and ability to manage affect are affected.

The psychological distress stemming from maltreatment produces avoidance responses, including dissociation and tension-reducing activities. Due to impairment in self-functioning, the individual is easily overwhelmed by trauma-related affects, resulting in further avoidance and disruption in the development of self-capacities. The re-experiencing of fragments of the trauma through intrusive symptomatology are attempts to accommodate the trauma. Due to dissociation, however, the individual does not experience the exposure to the traumatic material needed for desensitization and resolution of chronic symptomatology. Briere concluded:

> This process may lead the abuse survivor in therapy to present as chronically dissociated, besieged by overwhelming yet unending intrusive symptomatology, and as having 'characterological' difficulties associated with identity, boundary, and affect regulation difficulties. (1996: 145)

A framework for male survivors

The symptom patterns of male survivors may be affected by socialization factors specific to gender and victimization. Struve (1990) has identified nine factors that may have an impact on the presentation of the male survivor. These nine factors are:

1 reluctance to seek treatment due to the beliefs that men are not victims and, if they are, that they are less traumatized by the victimizing experience than are females;
2 minimization of the experience of victimization due to the belief that sexual activity with an older woman is a privilege and that victimization by a male reflects one's own sexual orientation;
3 shame-based personality dynamics based on one's perceived failure to protect oneself or to achieve appropriate revenge against the offender;
4 exaggerated efforts to reassert masculine identity in an attempt to compensate for the failure to protect oneself;
5 difficulties with male identity resulting in the avoidance of any behaviours perceived as feminine, including emotional intimacy with other males;
6 confusion about sexual identity due to one's perceived passivity or sexual arousal experienced during same-sex abuse;
7 behaviour patterns with power/control dynamics due to attempts to overcompensate for the powerlessness experienced during the abuse;
8 externalization of feelings due to social prescriptions that males can act on, but not express, their feelings;
9 vulnerability to compulsive behaviours due to attempts to deny feelings by excessive involvement with 'product- and task-oriented activities' (1990: 38).

The framework indicates that male survivors may be even more likely than females to avoid treatment or disclosure and to minimize their abuse experience. Males will often present with behavioural (e.g. negative consequences of aggression), rather than emotionally expressive (e.g. complaints of depression), issues. A 'disguised' presentation may include exaggerated masculine or 'macho' behaviours, difficulties with intimacy with males, sexual identity confusion, aggressive or controlling behaviours, and compulsive behaviours.

Counselling issues

When discussing the counselling of adult survivors of childhood sexual abuse, several basic issues or questions arise. Although there are no definitive answers to these questions, each will be addressed in turn.

Counsellor qualifications

Many counsellors ask whether the unique needs of the adult survivor require that he or she be seen by a sexual abuse 'specialist', a professional who works with adult survivors as a primary clinical focus. If we continue to find that a large percentage of individuals who seek counselling have had some experience of childhood sexual victimization, it is unlikely that all of these clients can be seen by a 'specialist'. Although it is important for counsellors to recognize that survivors' needs are unique and complex, to suggest that they need to see a 'specialist' might convey the message that their needs are extremely complicated or unusual – thereby increasing their sense of isolation and their view of themselves as being different.

Counsellors do need to develop skills and competencies to meet the needs of survivors effectively. For example, the development of self-awareness regarding one's attitudes and beliefs related to the issue of childhood sexual abuse is essential. As mentioned earlier, helping professionals come from a tradition of denial of the reality and prevalence of childhood sexual abuse. This reflects deeper societal values regarding gender roles, power issues, and the rights of children. Counsellors need to examine their own values and attitudes that could interfere with effective counselling (e.g. denial, disgust, blaming the victim). They must also question whether they accept any myths that research and clinical experience have consistently disproved. Hall and Lloyd (1989) have outlined several commonly accepted myths related to sexual abuse. These myths include the following: sexual abuse occurs only in certain subgroups of the population (e.g. poor, isolated families), if a child does nothing to stop the abuse he or she must therefore have welcomed it, and mothers often 'collude' with the abuser and so share responsibility for the abuse.

In addition to evaluating their beliefs and attitudes, counsellors need training and supervision in counselling adult survivors. A counsellor who is inexperienced in dealing with this clinical issue needs to develop and maintain competencies as one would when faced with any special clinical concern (e.g. treating substance abuse or counselling individuals from varied cultural backgrounds). Training can include classroom or workshop instruction and supervised clinical experience. Because counselling survivors is an intensely emotional experience that can provoke numerous personal issues, supervision or professional consultation is recommended even for counsellors who are experienced in this area.

The counsellor's gender

Another question that frequently arises is whether counsellors should be of the same gender as the survivors with whom they are working. Some clinicians have concluded that, at least initially, a female counsellor is preferable for female survivors. Faria and Belohlavek (1984) suggested that while a male therapist would allow survivors to learn to develop healthy relationships with men, a female counsellor is preferable as she can serve as a role model. Blake-White and Kline (1985) argued that female therapists are more effective as leaders of incest therapy groups because it is usually easier for survivors to trust women. These authors also suggested that introducing a male co-therapist at a later point could benefit the group by providing the survivors with an opportunity to explore their attitudes toward men. While Hall and Lloyd (1989) identified the advantages of a female counsellor, they also acknowledged that a male counsellor provides survivors with an opportunity to establish a healthy relationship with a male. Others have maintained that the gender of the counsellor is not a significant issue. For example, Westerlund (1983) emphasized that counselling style is more influential than the gender of the counsellor in determining how issues of power are handled within the relationship.

Less has been written regarding the gender of counsellors working with male survivors. Bruckner and Johnson (1987) recommended the use of mixed-gender co-leaders for male survivor groups because having a female present can facilitate the discussion of issues and feelings. Evans (1990: 71), who discussed the treatment of male sexual assault survivors and Vietnam veterans, stated that 'The key issue in gender identification with the client . . . is not the gender of the client and the survivor but the gender attitudes'. The ability of counsellors to examine their own gender-related issues, and the ways in which power issues are handled within the counselling relationship, therefore, may ultimately be more important than the gender mix between counsellor and client.

The gender of the client

A commonly raised question is how the counselling needs of males differ from those of females. Because many female and male responses to childhood sexual abuse are similar (e.g. guilt, shame, anger), many counselling processes and techniques to be discussed in this book are applicable to both genders. Because the socialization of males and females differs, however, it can be expected that males will be confronted with different sexist biases, exhibit gender-specific presentations of symptoms, and have specific treatment needs (Draucker and Petrovic, 1996, 1997; Hunter and Gerber, 1990).

In their review of the initial and long-term effects of childhood sexual abuse on boys, Urquiza and Capra (1990) cited several effects that were similar to those experienced by women and girls (e.g. self-concept disturbance, somatic complaints), but identified two areas that 'stood out' for males: disturbances of conduct and acting out of compulsive sexual behaviours. The authors suggested that these effects are related to gender-based differences in coping with trauma – most specifically, the use of externalizing behaviours by males.

Counsellors of male survivors, therefore, need to be sensitive to gender-specific issues. As Sepler (1990) pointed out, male victims inevitably experience their abuse from a different world view and self-view than do females. The crisis experienced by the male survivor related to the abuse 'may be unresponsive to, or further precipitated by, a programme model that assumes universality when it comes to sexual victimization' (1990: 76). By failing to acknowledge the male's view and by working from a model of victimization based primarily on women's experiences, counsellors could increase the male survivor's sense of isolation and alienation (Draucker and Petrovic, 1996, 1997).

Abuse by members of the same sex

A closely related issue is that of same-sex versus opposite-sex abuse. Whereas girls are most frequently victimized by men, boys are most frequently abused by other males. In addition to addressing the impact of socialization on males' responses to victimization, the issue of same-sex abuse is pertinent. The most frequently discussed specific effect arising from the experience of male-to-male abuse is confusion related to sexual identity. Struve (1990) pointed out that if the abused boy perceives himself as experiencing pleasure or sexual arousal, which are normal physiological responses to stimulation, he may interpret those reactions as latent homosexual feelings; this can lead to later identity confusion. The male survivor often directs anger towards himself for not protecting himself from another male, and therefore views himself as unmanly (Struve, 1990). His attempts to overcompensate for this failure may result in exaggerated 'macho behaviours', homophobia, sexually aggressive behaviours, and, in some cases, sexual offending.

Abuse by females

Little is known about abuse of both males and females by female offenders. Kasl (1990) suggested that the prevalence of childhood sexual abuse by female offenders is higher than originally believed. Finkelhor and Russell (1984) estimated that approximately 24 per cent of male victims and 13 per cent of female victims are abused by females. These females were often acting in conjunction with another offender. The under-reporting of abuse by females, especially in intra-familial situations, might be due to society's tendency to view males as aggressors and females as victims, or to possible differences in the types of offence committed by female offenders. Offences by female offenders may be less overt and embedded in typical parenting behaviours (e.g. caressing the child while bathing him or her, becoming sexual with a child while 'cuddling' in bed).

Because so little is known about abuse by female offenders, it is premature to identify any specific counselling needs of survivors. In many situations, however, it is believed that abuse by females is male-coerced and often accompanied by sexual and emotional abuse by both parents (Matthews et al., 1990). It is likely that the counselling needs of these survivors are quite complex.

Another scenario of abuse by females involves the extra-familial abuse of a younger male by an older woman, such as that between teacher and student. Often each party considers this to be a 'love affair'. Due to cultural influences, the male might not consider his experience abusive, but may experience long-term effects that he does not understand. Denial would be a significant counselling issue in this instance.

Structure of book

This book will discuss the counselling of adult survivors of child-hood sexual abuse by identifying significant healing processes thought to be necessary for recovery. These processes include disclosing the abuse, focusing on the abuse experience, reinter-preting the abuse from an adult perspective, addressing issues related to the context of the abuse, making desired life changes, and dealing with abuse resolution issues. As each of these processes is discussed, counselling interventions that facilitate resolution will be outlined.

The individual counselling relationship will be emphasized, although a chapter will be devoted to group counselling. The book will discuss issues and interventions that are applicable to varied types of childhood sexual abuse (e.g. same-sex and opposite-sex abuse, abuse of males and females). An effort will be made, however, to avoid the assumption of 'universality' (Sepler, 1990) by addressing significant differences between abuse experiences, when applicable.

Specific relationship combinations of offenders and survivors (e.g. father–daughter, brother–sister, stranger–child) will not be addressed separately. Although the impact of the relationship between the victim and the offender is significant, relationship vari-ables are complex; factors other than the formal relationship between the two may be important, including the emotional closeness or amount of authority possessed by the offender. Most survivors who seek treatment as adults are dealing with abuse that occurred in the context of their intimate social world and this will be the primary focus of the book.

In most instances, case examples described and interventions recommended are drawn from the author's clinical and research experiences with survivors. To ensure anonymity of individual clients and research participants, all names are changed and identifying facts are disguised. To further protect confidentiality, some clinical examples are actually composites of several cases.

When the client referred to is an adult who was abused as a child, the term 'survivor' will be used to avoid the connotations associated with the label of victim. When the client is a child who is experiencing abuse, the term 'victim' will be used to emphasize his or her inability to consent to the sexual activity. In all cases, clients who are dealing with childhood sexual abuse are con-sidered individuals who have shared a common traumatic experi-ence, but who have unique needs, desires, and strengths.

The False Memory Debate:
Counselling Implications

C ounsellors who work with adult survivors of childhood
sexual abuse will undoubtedly confront issues raised by the
current controversy related to the phenomenon of recovered
memories, i.e. the recall of traumatic events not previously remembered. Courtois (1999: 81) has suggested that three issues comprise
the false memory debate: 'whether trauma can be forgotten and
then remembered, the accuracy and credibility of memories of CSA
[childhood sexual abuse], and the role of therapist influence on
memory'. One cadre of experts maintains that recovered memories
are confabulations that are typically iatrogenic in nature; that
is, they are induced by questionable therapeutic practices or the
self-help literature. This view is endorsed by the False Memory
Syndrome Foundation, a well-funded coalition of parents accused
of abuse by their adult children and professionals who question
the phenomenon of recovered memories. Opponents of this view
maintain that recovered memories are typically accurate and
should not be met with scepticism by clinicians. The counselling
implications of the controversy will be discussed.

Trauma theory

Theories regarding the nature of traumatic memories are the basis
for many counselling processes used with adult survivors of childhood sexual abuse, and are at the root of the false memory debate.
Traumatologists argue that memories of traumatic experiences,
defined as overwhelming events outside of the realm of normal
experience, are encoded, stored, and retrieved differently than are
memories for ordinary events (Horowitz, 1976; Janet, 1925/1976;
van der Kolk and van der Hart, 1991). Because traumatic memories
do not fit existing cognitive schemata, they may not be integrated
with ordinary verbal autobiographical memory or incorporated in
one's conscious self-representation (Brown et al., 1998).

Traumatic memory loss is best understood as one type of defensive dissociation. Braun (1988) identified four parameters of experience: behaviour, affect, somatic sensation, and knowledge. When an individual experiences a traumatic event, these parameters of experience can become disconnected (dissociated) as a defence against overwhelming affect. Defensive dissociation may include numbing (separation of feelings from awareness of current events), derealization (sense of detachment from surroundings), depersonalization (sense of detachment from one's body), and dissociative amnesia (inability to recall events or periods of time). Dissociative identity disorder (DID) involves a sense of internal fragmentation of the self (Chu, 1998). Post-traumatic stress disorder (PTSD) involves a numbing phase (the dissociation of traumatic events from cognitive awareness) that alternates with an intrusive phase (the return of awareness of traumatic events through thoughts, dreams, and flashbacks). The severity of the dissociative symptoms seems to be associated with the severity of the early trauma (Chu). Repression, the involuntary, selective forgetting of material that causes pain (Holmes, 1990), is, therefore, only one manifestation of dissociation associated with traumatic experiences.

Most trauma experts believe that traumatic memories are less malleable than ordinary memories because they are not subjected to the same processing mechanisms, such as transformations, deletions, and insertions. Dissociated traumatic memories can nonetheless implicitly influence consciousness and return intrusively as fragmentary sensory or motor experiences (Brown et al., 1998). Because the storage of traumatic memories is state- or context-dependent, memories can be triggered by situations reminiscent of the original trauma (contextual cues) or by emotional and physiological arousal or sensory stimulation associated with the trauma (state cues). Retrieved traumatic memories are often accompanied by intense physiological arousal and affective distress. Recovery from trauma involves the transformation of traumatic memories into narrative language and the integration of such memories into existing mental schemata. Brown et al. (1998: 440) concluded that: 'to the extent that traumatic memory remains dissociated, the basic assumption guiding treatment is the integration of dissociated memory components'.

The false memory perspective

False memory proponents question the basic tenets of trauma theory – most specifically, the concept of repression. They often cite a critical review of the research literature by Holmes (1990), who concluded that there is little scientific validation of the existence of repression, and challenge clinical reports indicating that a large percentage of survivors of childhood trauma suffer from some degree of amnesia. Much of the false memory argument is based on laboratory research that demonstrates the malleability of human memory (Lindsay and Read, 1994).

One line of research has investigated the misleading information effect. In a typical experimental paradigm, subjects are asked to witness pictures, slides, or videotapes of an event in a laboratory setting, are given misleading suggestions or questions regarding some details of the event, and are tested on their memories of the event. In many experiments, subjects report events or details consistent with the misleading information (Lindsay, 1990, 1994; Weingardt et al., 1994). Some subjects express confidence in their illusory memories and provide vivid and detailed descriptions of inaccurate details.

Researchers have demonstrated that memory suggestibility for misleading post-event information is increased by several factors: delay between the event and attempts at recall; the perceived authority of the source of misleading information; repetition of false statements; plausible rather than implausible suggestions; and the use of lax memory-monitoring criteria, such as being asked to respond only with a 'yes' or a 'no' to memory items or being encouraged to guess (Lindsay and Read, 1994). In a similar paradigm, children are interrogated by adult interviewers about an event they have witnessed (Ceci and Bruck, 1993; Ceci et al., 1994). After repeated, misleading questioning, some children report events that never occurred. As the interrogation continues, they often provide increasing detail about the fictitious events.

Another line of research has demonstrated that individuals can be led to experience pseudo-memories of fabricated childhood events in the laboratory setting (Hyman et al., 1995; Hyman and Pentland, 1996). In several experiments by Hyman and colleagues, investigators interviewed parents of college students to gather data on the students' childhood experiences. The students were asked to recall several real life events and a fictitious event, having been told that information regarding all the events had been supplied by parents or close relatives. When the students were repeatedly interviewed about all events, about 25 per cent eventually recalled the fictitious event. Susceptibility to false recall was increased by the plausibility of the event, suggestions by the investigator that mental practice (imagining, reflection) would improve recall, repeated trials of remembering, and by certain cognitive and personality variables .

An often-cited example of confabulation of real life events is drawn from a study involving a 14-year-old boy named Chris (Loftus, 1993). In a laboratory experiment, Jim, Chris' older brother, helped construct a fabricated childhood story that he then told to Chris. Chris was told that at the age of five he had been separated from his family at a shopping mall and was later found crying in the presence of an older man, who said that he was trying to help Chris find his parents. In addition to recalling the incident, on subsequent days Chris began to describe it more vividly, expanding on details originally provided by Jim. When told about the deception, Chris had difficulty believing that the event never occurred.

Research has also demonstrated that individuals may mistake memories of imagined events for real events, especially when the memories were formed during childhood (Lindsay and Read, 1994). Mentally rehearsing such events makes recollections more vivid and detailed. Individual differences may affect memory distortions. Individuals who are field dependent (rely heavily on environmental cues for perceptual judgements), depressed, or hypnotizable may be especially vulnerable to memory distortion (Lindsay and Read, 1994).

Drawing on these experimental data, false memory proponents suggest that certain therapeutic techniques aimed at memory recovery and self-help strategies for survivors of childhood trauma run the risk of implanting false memories in vulnerable individuals. Lindsay and Read, for example, suggested that,

> For present purposes, the important point is that many of the factors that memory researchers have found contribute to the likelihood of illusory memories (e.g. perceived authority of the source of sugges- tions, repetition of suggestions, communication of information that heightens the plausibility of the suggestions, encouragement to form images of suggested events and to reduce criteria for the acceptance of current mental experiences as memories) are typical of memory recovery therapies. (1994: 294)

Therapists and authors of self-help literature who suggest to individuals that they are 'likely' to have been sexually abused on the basis of suggestive histories and/or symptom profiles have been challenged by false memory proponents (Loftus, 1993). The incest book industry is heavily criticized, especially the popular book *The courage to heal* (Bass and Davis, 1994). Loftus questioned 'suggestions to readers that they were likely abused even if there are no memories, that repressed memories of abuse undoubtedly underlie one's troubles, or that benefits derive from uncovering repressed memories and believing them' (1993: 525). Loftus also criticized therapists who use intrusive probing to assess for a history of childhood sexual abuse or who persist in interrogating a client after the client indicates that he or she was not abused in childhood.

Specific therapeutic techniques, such as hypnosis, that are used to provoke or enhance repressed memories of childhood sexual abuse, are the most suspect. Observers argue that individuals who experience vague or weak images under hypnosis are likely to report them as actual memories and, when in a waking state, they feel confident that these memories are accurate (Lindsay and Read, 1994). Similarly, procedures using guided imagery may place a client at risk of mistaking imagined events for actual occurrences. Proponents of the false memory perspective also object to therapeutic strategies that use uncritical free association, instructions to guess about past events, interpretation of suggestive dreams as unconscious messages about childhood sexual abuse, and interpretations of physical symptoms as 'body memories' of childhood sexual abuse (Lindsay and Read, 1994; Loftus, 1993). Survivor groups for individuals who have no abuse memories are criticized because such groups often reinforce the telling of abuse narratives and encourage members to assume the 'survivor' role. Madden (1998) warned that the following techniques have been associated with the creation of false memories in legal proceedings: guided imagery, age regression, journalling, dream work and interpretation, eye movement desensitization and reprocessing (EMDR), art therapy, feelings/emotional release work, group therapy, and bibliotherapy.

The rebuttal

The false memory perspective has been criticized on several grounds. Conte (1999) challenged the argument that there is no scientific evidence for the existence of repression. He argued that Holmes' (1990) review focused only on laboratory research and pointed out that Holmes himself stressed that the lack of empirical evidence for regression should not be interpreted as suggesting that repression does not exist; only that it has not been proven in the laboratory. Based on the results of several clinical studies (Briere and Conte, 1993; Cameron, 1994; Gold et al., 1994; Herman and Schatzow, 1987), several experts have argued that some degree of amnesia is relatively common among adult survivors of childhood trauma (Chu, 1998; Harvey, 1999). In a study conducted by Williams (1994), for example, 38 per cent of 129 women who had childhood abuse experiences that were documented by medical and social service records did not recall these events during an interview 17 years later.

Conte (1999) critiqued laboratory research findings related to the misinformation effect. He argued that much of this research involves subjects who have no personal investment in events to be remembered, provides no data indicating how much effort is needed to produce what effect or whether misinformation effects are resistant to change, and does not address what intrapersonal factors (IQ, stress level, emotional state) increase susceptibility to the effect. Conte also pointed out that the rate of error in these experiments tends to be low (less than 20 per cent). He recommended that future memory researchers focus on events more similar to actual abuse and trauma incidents and involve individuals more similar to those likely to be affected by memory issues – for example those seeking psychotherapy for help with anxiety, depression, or other troubling emotions.

Research findings related to the creation of pseudo-memories have also been questioned because the responses of the subjects in these experiments are likely to be influenced by the expectations of the investigator (Conte, 1999). Additionally, subjects are given information supposedly provided by individuals who should have the most accurate knowledge about their childhood – i.e. their own parents and close relatives.

Finally, Conte challenged the conclusions of false memory proponents that certain therapy techniques create false memories. He cautioned that there is no research evidence to support criticisms that guided imagery, journalling, dream interpretation, and survivor groups produce false memories of childhood sexual abuse.

Implications for counsellors

Several experts have called for a middle ground response to the controversy – a reasoned, balanced perspective that is informed by emerging information on the complex topic of traumatic memory (Brown et al., 1998; Chu, 1998; Courtois, 1999). Recommendations for counsellors who work with clients who have sustained trauma, especially regarding memory issues, have been proposed. There is general consensus that counsellors should operate from a broad knowledge base and maintain an 'open, reflective and neutral' (Courtois, 1999: 271) stance regarding memory issues, recognizing that memory is fluid, malleable, and reconstructive. Counsellors who work with trauma survivors must stay current with the rapid proliferation of knowledge related to trauma and memory, and must have specialized training and competence to use specific memory enhancement techniques. Ongoing supervision, consultation, and periodic review of treatment plans are crucial.

Brown et al. (1998) argued that the term 'memory recovery therapy' is a misnomer for contemporary trauma treatment in so far as the primary goal of treatment is rarely memory retrieval. Trauma therapy typically has a number of treatment foci. Memory enhancement may be one component of treatment and is used only when indicated (as discussed on page 47). Memory work should always serve the purpose of integration; that is, trauma-related symptoms and behavioural re-enactments are translated into a coherent narrative for the purpose of finding meaning in one's history and gaining mastery of the trauma (Brown et al., 1998). Counsellors should always conduct a comprehensive assessment that focuses on a multitude of life issues and should develop a comprehensive and integrated treatment plan addressing all issues, not just those related to abuse.

An assessment for risk of false memory production is indicated before beginning any memory work (Brown et al. 1998; Courtois, 1999). The following client characteristics may indicate susceptibility: high level of hypnotizability or interrogatory suggestibility, certain personality factors (immaturity, dependence, external locus of control) or disorders (hysteria, borderline, antisocial), depression, and dissociative states. Counsellors should ascertain what memories clients have of childhood trauma when treatment begins to provide a baseline for any later memory work.

Counsellors should neither unequivocally validate nor automatically disbelieve recovered or continuous trauma memories presented by clients in therapy. Free narrative recall, in which clients are encouraged to discuss thoughts, feelings, and experiences in response to open-ended, non-suggestive questioning, often yields significant information about past events without increasing the risk of memory error (Brown et al., 1998). Often, even in instances of full or partial amnesia, no special memory enhancement techniques are required. Gold and Brown (1997: 186) stated: 'when clients are allowed to develop sufficient coping abilities and trust in therapy relationships, recall of previously traumatic material will occur relatively spontaneously, without leading or prodding'. Client-driven recall fosters a sense of control and mastery.

Counsellors, therefore, should avoid leading or close-ended questions, premature conclusions, and uncritical acceptance of memories as historical truths. Techniques thought to cause the greatest risk of suggestibility should be used with caution and only with proper training. Regressive techniques and the use of hypnosis for memory retrieval are generally discouraged (Brown et al., 1998; Courtois, 1999).

Informed consent is an important aspect of trauma work, especially when memory issues are involved. Each client should be provided with information alerting him or her to the general office policies and procedures (e.g. payment for services, the limits of confidentiality, interactions with third party payers). The basic elements, parameters, and risks and benefits of counselling in general should be discussed (Madden, 1998). If memory integration may be a component of treatment, accurate and detailed information regarding the nature of memory and memory retrieval should be provided. Brown et al. (1998) recommend that clients be informed that memories contain a blend of accurate and inaccurate information and that even memories that are emotionally compelling may be inaccurate with respect to historical truth. Common errors in memory, such as detail reconstruction, source misattribution, and confabulation, should be discussed. If any specialized memory enhancement interventions are used, specific information should be provided regarding the anticipated duration and cost, the advantages and disadvantages, and available alternatives. Possible risks should be clearly delineated.

The impact of counselling on third parties has also received closer scrutiny due to the false memory controversy. Trauma clinicians are advised to refrain from recommending that clients separate from family members who have abused or wronged them. If a current family relationship presents a danger, the counsellor may assist the client in determining the steps needed to ensure safety (Courtois, 1999). If a family member is invited to a treatment session, counsellors should be aware that this might imply a professional treatment relationship – and, therefore, a duty owed – to that person (Brown et al., 1998). Several experts have also stressed that it is inappropriate for a counsellor to recommend litigation (Brown et al., 1998; Courtois, 1999). If clients opt to instigate a lawsuit, the counsellor should help them explore their thoughts and feelings related to this choice and gather pertinent information regarding the legal process. Brown et al. argued that 'therapists should caution adult patients against impulsive actions of any kind based on information uncovered in psychotherapy or hypnotherapy, encouraging them to thoughtfully and critically evaluate this material for a substantial period of time, as well as consider potential negative consequences of confrontation or disclosure of this information' (1998: 503).

Thorough documentation of clinical work with trauma survivors is critical (Brown et al., 1998; Courtois, 1999). Counsellors' records should reflect that they have discussed the dynamics of memory, including issues of adequacy and completeness, with clients for whom abuse memories may be a pertinent issue. All notes should reflect a neutral and objective stance regarding the accuracy of recovered memories. For example, the records should indicate that the counsellor avoided suggestive influence, critically evaluated memories retrieved in therapy, and refrained from encouraging impulsive actions that might be injurious to third parties. When techniques with a high risk of suggestibility are used, detailed documentation should accompany each procedure.

Phase-oriented treatment

The controversy has prompted trauma clinicians to develop a standard of care for trauma treatment and to identify acceptable practice parameters (Madden, 1998). Numerous experts agree that a phase-oriented treatment is the most acceptable approach for working with trauma victims, including adult survivors of childhood sexual abuse. Phase-oriented treatment 'divides the overall treatment into discrete phases or stages of treatment, each with its own treatment objectives or goals' (Brown et al., 1998: 437). There is much consensus in the literature regarding the stages, nature, and goals of treatment. Several authors describe an early phase of treatment that focuses on stabilization and mastery, including building the therapeutic relationship, attenuation and containment of stress-related symptomatology, establishing safety, and coping with current life problems. The second phase typically involves the integration of traumatic memories, whether by acknowledging and validating remembered trauma or by enhancing memory in cases of amnesia. A final phase often focuses on self-development, relational development, or adaptation to daily life. Three examples of phase-oriented treatment models applicable to adult survivors of childhood sexual abuse are presented in Table 2.1.

Table 2.1 *Phase-oriented treatment models for adult survivors of childhood sexual abuse*

Author	Phase		
	I	II	III
Courtois (1999)	Early phase • establishment of treatment parameters • development of therapeutic relationship and working alliance • maintenance of personal safety and relative life stability • development of additional sources of support • attention to self-functions and symptom management skills	Middle phase • deconditioning (graduated and controlled exposure to traumatic material) • mourning • resolution and integration of trauma	Late phase • self and relational development • life reconsolidation and restructuring
Herman (1992)	Establishing safety • naming the problem through diagnostic evaluation • restoring control of body • establishing a safe environment	Remembrance and mourning • reconstructing the story • transforming traumatic memory • mourning traumatic loss	Reconnection • learning to fight (taking power in real life situations) • reconciling with oneself • reconnecting with others • finding a survivor mission • resolving the trauma
Chu (1998)	Early-stage treatment • self-care • symptom control • acknowledgment of trauma • functioning • expression of affect • establishing mutual and collaborative relationships	Middle-stage treatment (abreaction) • increased symptomatology • intense internal conflict • acceptance and mourning • mobilization and empowerment	Late-stage treatment • consolidation of gains • increasing skills in creating healthy interactions with outside world

3

Disclosing an Experience of Child Sexual Abuse

Inquiry about childhood sexual abuse

Inquiry about early trauma, including childhood sexual abuse, should occur in the context of an ongoing, comprehensive assessment. Such an assessment should include: discussion of the presenting problem(s); identification of clinical signs, symptoms, and diagnostic indicators; a social, personal, treatment, legal, and financial history; and evaluation of personality factors, including strengths and assets, that may influence the course of treatment (Courtois, 1999).

Some counsellors may hesitate to ask about childhood sexual abuse during an initial assessment due to fear of creating unnecessary distress for the client ('opening a can of worms') or concern that such questioning may be too suggestive. Most experts agree, however, that routine inquiry about childhood sexual abuse, as well as other experiences of current and past violence, should be conducted in an open-ended, non-judgmental, and straightforward manner. Gelinas (1983: 326) stated:

> Although patients find it paralysingly difficult to disclose spontaneously, they will almost invariably disclose after specific inquiry by the therapist. In response to such inquiries patients have broken silences of up to 56 years. Inquiry by the therapist implies permission to talk of such things and signals the therapist's ability to tolerate the anxiety such a discussion might generate.

Courtois (1999) recommended asking about childhood sexual abuse in terms that are descriptive and behavioural. It may not be helpful, for example, to ask clients if they ever experienced 'sexual abuse' because individuals differ as to what they consider sexual or abusive. More effective questions might be:

1 As a child, were you ever touched in a way that felt uncomfortable (embarrassing, frightening) to you?

2   As a child, did anyone ever ask you to do something sexual, such as . . .?
3   As a child, did anyone hurt you or use you in a sexual way?

These questions may be coupled with a more traditional psychosexual history (e.g. 'Tell me about your first sexual experience'; 'How did you learn about sex?'). Discussion of clients' retrospective views of their childhood sexual experiences will determine whether they considered these experiences harmful, even if they do not label them as sexual abuse. In addition to asking when the client's first sexual experience occurred, for example, it is helpful to ask how he or she felt about this and subsequent sexual experiences.

Josephson and Fong-Beyette (1987) researched factors associated with disclosure of incest in counselling. They interviewed 37 female incest survivors who had been to a counsellor; those survivors who had disclosed their sexual abuse to the counsellor indicated that they did so because they believed that they would feel better, because a media piece or others encouraged them to do so, or because the counsellor had directly inquired about the incest. Those who did not disclose the sexual abuse to their counsellor reported that they were not thinking about the incest, did not believe it was related to their present concerns, or considered their present concerns to be more important. In addition, they reported that their counsellors did not ask about childhood sexual abuse. These authors recommended that counsellors can elicit disclosure by directly questioning clients about childhood sexual, emotional, and physical abuse, along with more general questioning related to the quality of childhood experiences and family relationships (e.g. the client's best and worst childhood experiences).

Standardized assessment

Briere (1997) reviewed five standardized instruments used to assess childhood abuse histories. These instruments are: (1) the Assessing Environments III (AEIII), Form SD (Rausch and Knutson, 1991); (2) the Childhood Trauma Questionnaire (CTQ, Bernstein et al., 1994); (3) the Child Maltreatment Interview Schedule (CMIS, Briere, 1992); (4) the Childhood Maltreatment Questionnaire (CMQ, Demaré, 1993); and (5) the Traumatic Events Scale (TES, Elliot, 1992).

In addition, several instruments have been developed to measure symptoms related to childhood abuse. These instruments are: (1) the Impact of Event Scale (IES, Horowitz et al., 1979); (2) the Dissociative Experiences Scale (DES, Bernstein and Putnam, 1986); (3) the Los Angeles Symptom Checklist (LASC, Foy et al., 1984); (4) the Trauma Symptom Checklist-40 (TSC-40, Elliott and Briere, 1992); and (5) the Trauma Symptom Inventory (TSI, Briere, 1995; Elliott and Briere, 1995). Briere cautioned, however, that these instruments have been primarily used in research and need further development and testing prior to widespread clinical application. Because the long-term effects of childhood sexual abuse are so variable, a symptom checklist alone is not sufficient to make a definite determination of abuse.

Traditional personality inventories (e.g. the Minnesota Multi-phasic Personality Inventory Manual [MMPI], Hathaway and McKinley, 1967; the Millon Clinical Multi-axial Inventory III [MCMI–III], Millon, 1994) are often used in the assessment of survivors who present for treatment. Although these instruments may be used to assess personality characteristics (e.g. impulsiveness) or acute clinical states (e.g. suicidality), they cannot detect a history of childhood sexual abuse. For example, certain MMPI profiles and the endorsement of certain critical items have been frequently reported in clinical samples of sexual abuse survivors, but the same patterns have also been found in non-survivor samples (Briere, 1989). At this point, there is no specific profile for sexual abuse that has been identified for any standardized personality instrument.

Factors such as suggestibility and hynotizability, which are associated with risk of pseudo-memory production, should be evaluated, especially if memory work is likely (Brown et al., 1998; Courtois, 1999). The use of standardized instruments (e.g. the Hypnotic Induction Profile [Spiegal and Spiegal, 1987], the Gudjonsson Suggestibility Scale [Gudjonsson, 1984]) is recommended for this purpose.

Undisclosed sexual abuse histories

Despite a comprehensive assessment, many individuals with a history of childhood sexual abuse do not disclose these experiences to the counsellor. In some cases, survivors may recall their abuse experiences and recognize their significance, but choose not to talk about the experiences because they do not yet trust the counsellor. Other survivors with memories of childhood sexual abuse may not disclose their experiences because they do not believe that the abuse played a significant role in their lives. These individuals often claim that they did not bring up the abuse initially because they believed it was 'in the past' or 'no big deal'. Such minimization may be especially pronounced in male survivors, as gender socialization often inhibits males from viewing themselves as victims. Frequently, the lack of disclosure is related to a process of 'protective denial' (Sgroi, 1989a). As discussed earlier, defensive dissociation is a common response to childhood trauma and clients may experience varying degrees of dissociative amnesia. These clients do not disclose their abuse experiences because they do not have clear memories of them.

Counsellors should not make assumptions regarding lack of disclosure; it may simply mean that no abuse occurred. Under certain conditions, however, counsellors need to consider that the client may have experienced childhood trauma, including childhood sexual abuse. Courtois suggested:

> When the individual's symptom picture is acute and/or has a strong resemblance to complex dissociative PTSD . . . or when the therapist observes certain behavioral and response patterns commonly associated with trauma (such as dissociation in the session or a high degree of personal risk-taking, substance abuse, chronic self-harm and suicidality, and/or a history of re-victimization), the possibility of undisclosed or unrecognized abuse or other trauma or forms of abuse that often go unrecognized (extreme neglect, attachment abuse, or emotional abuse) should be considered. (1999: 229)

Counsellors may consider familial risk factors in addition to symptomatology when considering the possibility of abuse (Brown et al., 1998). Research has shown that the following factors are associated with child sexual abuse: being female, being a preadolescent or early adolescent, living without a natural parent, having an impaired mother, poor parenting, or witnessing family conflict (Finkelhor, 1993). Finkelhor has stressed, however, that 'none of these factors bear a strong enough relationship to the occurrence of abuse that their presence could play a confirming or disconfirming role in the identification of actual cases' (1993: 67).

When a sexual abuse history is not disclosed, counsellors should not 'diagnose' repressed memory or undetected sexual abuse; they may, however, formulate an 'index of suspicion' based on the factors identified above. Brown et al. stated:

> Our confidence level in suspecting genuine abuse is raised when the patient presents with: signs and symptoms consistent with abuse; five or greater family history risk factors associated with abuse; clear evidence of dissociation; and no evidence of being in the high range of hypnotic or memory suggestibility. (1998: 508)

Even when abuse is strongly suspected, but not known, the counsellor should neither speculate about nor confirm past sexual abuse when responding to the client. The counsellor should refrain from attributing all the client's problems and concerns to any single aetiology, including childhood sexual abuse (Brown et al., 1998; Courtois, 1999). If the counsellor has a high index of suspicion and believes it is in the client's best interest to communicate this, he or she should do so tentatively, exploring other aetiological possibilities as well.

Counsellor's responses to disclosure

The counsellor's initial response to the client's disclosure of childhood sexual abuse is extremely important. If disclosure is not handled skilfully by the counsellor, it can have deleterious effects. If clients perceive the counsellor's response to disclosure as non-supportive, they may leave counselling, resist further discussion of the abuse issue, or minimize the impact of their abuse experience (Josephson and Fong-Beyette, 1987). Non-supportive responses may include: not believing clients who reveal a history of childhood abuse, blaming the client for the abuse, asking intrusive or voyeuristic questions related to the abuse, or minimizing the importance of the abuse.

In a qualitative study of the healing process of incest survivors (Draucker, 1992b), several participants reported that one of the most destructive counsellor responses to disclosure is that of shock, termed by the survivors as 'oh, my God' or 'jaw drop' responses. Although counsellors may perceive such intense reactions to be empathic or genuine, given the client's history, such responses may exacerbate the clients' feelings of stigma and isolation. One survivor in this study stated:

A lot of what happens for an incest survivor is very threatening to people who haven't been through it, and any kind of disbelief or shock or 'Oh, my God' you know, that kind of judgement is very damaging to me. One of the things that my first counsellor did at our first meeting was she just, her mouth dropped open and she just said, 'Oh, my God!' and I have just been telling her the basic things in my life.

Examples of non-helpful counsellor responses to disclosure may include:

1   Oh, my God. I can't believe anyone could actually do anything that horrible to a child. What your father did was disgusting. (shock response)

2 It sounds like you believe your father did these things to you. You were so young, it is hard to know what really happened. (disbelief)
3 Why did you agree to have sex with him? Why did you not tell your mother? Why did it go on for so long? (blaming)
4 You say that this experience is in the past and that you've coped with it. Why don't we move on then to the concerns you have today? (minimization)
5 Tell me exactly what he did to you sexually. (voyeuristic response)

Counsellors who reacted calmly but with 'appropriate concern' were perceived by the women in the incest healing study (Draucker, 1992b) to be both empathic and yet 'strong enough' to deal with the abuse issues. Supportive responses may include: acknowledging the difficult step of disclosing, offering support and indicating one's availability after the session during which the client disclosed, inviting the client to discuss the abuse at his or her own pace, and evaluating the client's mental status and determining any immediate safety concerns (e.g. suicidal thoughts).

Examples of helpful counsellor responses to disclosure may include:

1 I would like to hear more about that experience. Sexual abuse can be very painful for children and can continue to have an impact on one's life as an adult. (showing calm concern)
2 I can imagine it was hard for you to share that experience with me. I respect your courage for being able to do so. (acknowledging difficulty of disclosure)
3 It can be important to discuss your sexual abuse experience, as it may be related to your current concerns. However, we can do this at a pace that feels right to you. (reinforcing client's control of disclosure process)
4 For some women (men), sharing an abuse experience for the first time (with a counsellor) can result in some very strong (confusing, distressing) feelings. How are you feeling now? . . . Do you feel unsafe in any way? (acknowledging feelings, assessing safety)

Case example

The following case description exemplifies the process of an initial disclosure in counselling. Jean, a 34-year-old woman, was seen in a mental health centre following a family crisis in which her husband Jack, aged 42, was charged with physically abusing the couple's 16-year-old son, Bill. Bruises on Bill's arm had been noticed by a teacher and reported to the child protective agency, who referred the family for counselling. A family evaluation revealed that Jack had beaten Bill following an altercation regarding Bill's desire to leave school. The incident closely followed Jack's being fired from his job after a disagreement with his boss. Jack admitted to frequently using physical discipline (i.e. spanking) on his sons, but indicated that the most recent beating of Bill was the most serious. He stated that he lost control because of his drinking. The couple also had another son, Tom, aged 14, and a daughter, Sally, aged 12. All family members stated that Sally was never abused; they claimed she was always the 'good girl' who never did anything wrong and never needed any discipline.

Following the family evaluation, Jean was referred for individual therapy as she had revealed some vague suicidal ideation during the course of the meeting. She claimed that she was 'too tired' to deal with any more family problems, especially the fighting between Jack and Bill, and wished she 'never had to get out of bed again'. Jean was the oldest of eight children in her family. Her father was an alcoholic with a 'mean' temper who had worked at a local factory until his death several years earlier. He was physically abusive of his sons but had never hit Jean, who was always 'well behaved'. She described her mother as being a kind and gentle woman who was always sickly, but who 'waited on my father hand and foot'.

Jean married Jack when she was 17 because she saw marriage as a way of escaping her extensive responsibilities of caring for the younger children in the family. Also, Jack was 'pushing' her to marry shortly after high school graduation. Soon after they were married, Bill was born. Jean described the first year of Bill's life as the happiest time in her life. When she became pregnant with Tom, however, Jack began drinking heavily and would sometimes 'shove her around'. She explained that her husband demanded much of her attention. The drinking continued over the years, but Jack's abuse of her subsided. Jean stated that she never enjoyed their sex life. She eventually tried to avoid sex, although Jack would often demand it when he had been drinking.

Jean revealed that she had 'given up' on the boys. She would attempt to discipline them in a non-physical manner (e.g. by 'grounding them'), but they would not listen to her. Although Jean stated she was not close to either boy, she indicated that she was very close to Sally. She and Sally would often go shopping together and Sally would listen to her problems. Jean worked as a sales clerk at a local mall. She had started working on a college degree at a local community college on several occasions but stopped because of 'family responsibilities'. Shortly after Sally was born, Jean went to a psychiatrist and was treated for 'post-partum depression'. She was given antidepressant medication at that time.

Records revealed that Jack and Jean had been to the clinic for marriage counselling several years prior to the current crisis. A school guidance counsellor had recommended they seek help after Bill had got into several scraps with the law for petty theft and Tom, at age 11, had failed the fifth grade. It was recommended at that time that Jack attend Alcoholics Anonymous. Jean was diagnosed as having a dysthymic disorder and a dependent personality disorder. The couple discontinued counselling after three sessions, but Jean saw the counsellor individually for several more sessions. These sessions focused on her troubled marriage and on the behavioural problems of her sons.

Jean told her current counsellor that she was feeling depressed and admitted to feeling 'somewhat' suicidal at times. She said that she was spending every morning in bed. When the current crisis of Bill's beating occurred, she considered taking an overdose of some of her mother's 'nerve' pills but was 'too chicken' to do so. She stated she had lost over 10 pounds in two weeks. She denied any substance abuse herself. Her main complaint was: 'I'm just tired of it all and I want some peace.'

Assessment of Jean's presenting problem and history revealed that she exhibited several of the long-term effects frequently seen in adult survivors of abuse, including depression; low self-esteem and self-efficacy; general sexual dissatisfaction; an unsatisfactory marital relationship involving physical abuse and the alcoholism of her husband; and parenting difficulties. A history of parenti-fication, as described by Gelinas (1983), was evident. As the oldest of eight children, she had assumed many family responsibilities. Her father was a dependent, needy man who abused alcohol. Jean married a man with similar traits. She was unable to meet her own needs and began to show symptoms of depression after the birth of her third child, although she indicated that she was 'worn out' long before that time. Although there was no evidence that her daughter Sally had been sexually abused, Sally was experiencing parentification. At the age of 12, she had assumed the role of the responsible child and had become her mother's confidante.

Because of Jean's background and presenting symptoms, an assessment of a history of abuse was particularly important. Jean probably would not have revealed her abuse experiences to the counsellor unless directly asked. The following dialogue reflects the interaction between Jean and the counsellor that led to the disclosure that Jean had been sexually abused by her father. The disclosure occurred when the counsellor was inquiring about Jean's childhood experiences, and followed Jean's denial that she had been physically abused by her father.

Counsellor: You describe some difficult times in your childhood. Did anyone hurt you or use you in a sexual way?

Jean: Well, yes, I guess you could say so. I really don't like to talk about it. It's kind of embarrassing. It was my father. I guess it doesn't matter much now.

Counsellor: I realize this can be difficult to talk about. Oftentimes, sexual experiences in childhood are hurtful and can continue to influence women as adults. Therefore, it could be helpful for us to discuss it further. Would you be willing to do so?

Jean: Ya, I guess so. It happened so long ago, though. It wasn't like we really had sex or anything.

Counsellor: What did happen?

Jean: It would usually happen when he was drunk, which was not all the time. Maybe once a month or so. He would come into my room and feel me up – mostly my breasts, sometimes my private parts. It happened mostly when I was in junior high. [*Jean begins to cry.*] He would sometimes pass out in my bed but he always found his way back to his own by morning. I was afraid my mother would find out. It would have killed her. He stopped when I started to get interested in boys, I think. I really can't talk more about this any more. It's really my Billy that I'm concerned about.

Counsellor: I can sense it was hard for you to tell me about this. These are clearly painful memories. How are you feeling now?

Jean: Weird. I've never talked about it before. I guess I figured it is best to leave it dead and buried. It is so embarrassing, you know. I don't know, I feel kind of sad. I'll be OK, though. I do not think I can talk about my feelings any more. I'm not sure what they are. I have enough to deal with. Can we stop now?

Counsellor: Yes. Women often experience many different, and sometimes strong, feelings after sharing an experience such as yours. You may continue to experience these feelings when you leave here. Please feel free to contact me before we meet again if you are troubled by these feelings and want to talk. I also know you have been having some thoughts related to suicide . . . .

Jean: Yes, but like I said, I won't do anything.

Counsellor: If the thoughts get stronger or if you feel unsafe in any way, will you call me?

Jean: Yes. Will we talk about my father again next time? I don't think it will help with my problems with Jack or Bill, but I don't know.

Counsellor: Although it can be very difficult to deal with, I do recommend we discuss it further when you feel ready. Many of the things you are experiencing now, including your relationships with Bill and Tom, could be influenced by things you have experienced earlier in your life, including what happened with your father. We can explore these issues at a pace that feels right for you so that it will not seem so overwhelming. We would focus on how the abuse relates to your current problems, as it is these problems that trouble you now.

Jean: Maybe it is important. I've seen some movies about this kind of thing. I'll think some about it.

The counsellor initially intervened by acknowledging the difficulty of disclosure, validating the significance of the abuse, and inviting Jean to discuss it further. Counselling interventions were aimed at acknowledging the courage it took for Jean to discuss this experience, exploring her feelings, assessing her safety needs, and stressing the counsellor's availability. The counsellor also proposed a connection between this experience and Jean's current concerns and suggested that they explore the issue further at a pace that Jean controlled.

4

Focusing on the Abuse Experience

F ollowing disclosure, the counsellor and the client may decide to explore the sexual abuse as a significant counselling issue. The current standard of care in trauma treatment, the phase-oriented approach to therapy discussed in Chapter 2, calls for a preparatory or stabilization phase that precedes the exploration of traumatic memories. Depending on the client's initial presentation, this phase may involve a focus on symptom management, affect modulation and tolerance, cessation of self-injurious behaviours, control of addictions and compulsions, general self-care, and the formation of healthy relationships. The second phase of treatment involves exploring the abuse experience for the purpose of resolution and integration of the trauma. Both these phases are addressed in this chapter.

Preparing for exploration of childhood sexual abuse

Clients who present with severe, pervasive, and persistent symptoms may need considerable work in this initial phase; clients with well-developed self-capacities and support systems may start exploratory work relatively soon after beginning counselling. Adequate coping skills and psychosocial resources are crucial to the success of abuse-focused treatment. The task of developing coping and self-care techniques should be approached 'collaboratively and incrementally' (Gold and Brown, 1997: 187).

Chu (1998) stressed that although intensive exploration of abuse is contraindicated before stabilization is achieved, it is important to acknowledge the abuse at this stage. If early in treatment the counsellor does not acknowledge the influence of childhood trauma on the client's life, the client's denial may be exacerbated. Counsellors should, therefore, state that they consider the abuse a significant life experience but explain that it cannot be explored in greater depth until the client has certain resources and supports in place.

Managing trauma symptomatology

Many survivors of childhood sexual abuse are troubled by trauma-related symptoms (e.g. flashbacks, nightmares, perceptual disturbances) that may increase once the client begins to focus on the abuse experience. A temporary increase in trauma symptoms may be a necessary and therapeutic part of the healing process, representing the loosening of defences. As Sgroi (1989a: 116) has pointed out, the goal of treatment is 'not to suppress flashbacks or disturbing memories but rather to experience them and process them as a necessary step in coming to terms with and moving beyond the entire victimization experience'. It is advisable, however, to help the client develop skills to manage the symptoms prior to exploratory work, so that these symptoms do not become overwhelming.

Counsellors should explore the nature of the client's flashbacks, nightmares, and intrusive thoughts; acknowledge how frightening these symptoms can be; and assist clients in gaining control over them. Clients may be taught to identify circumstances that trigger intrusive symptomatology. Some clients experience certain prodromal experiences or emotional 'markers' (e.g. a sudden onset of depression) that precede the onset of intrusive symptomatology (Gold and Brown, 1997). If clients can identify these internal cues, they can develop responsive coping strategies. Such strategies may include contacting a supportive other or going to a physically safe place.

When clients re-experience past trauma, grounding techniques, i.e., strategies used to focus on current reality, can be useful (Blake-White and Kline, 1985; Cole and Barney, 1987; Meichenbaum, 1994). These strategies include physical methods (e.g. planting one's feet firmly on the ground or grasping the arms of one's chair during a flashback), or cognitive techniques (e.g. repeating one's name, age, and current location), to reinforce that one is not actually in the childhood situation. Clients may use an associational cue, an object that reminds them of safety and comfort, to maintain an awareness of current reality. They may also learn to find a 'safe space', either in actuality (e.g. the home of a trusted friend) or through imagery, to cope with intrusive symptoms (Meichenbaum, 1994). In a similar fashion, some clients can also learn to control the course of their nightmares. They may tell themselves before going to sleep, for example, that if they dream they are being chased by an intruder, they will stop and turn and order the intruder to leave – and he or she will do so.

Clients should be given the opportunity to discuss, process, and understand the aetiology and function of trauma symptoms

(Meichenbaum, 1994). Examining the messages about the trauma that are encoded in flashbacks or frightening dreams, for example, can help the client make sense of his or her symptoms. Meichenbaum stated, 'The client is encouraged to write, talk about, and even draw the experience so it shifts from a "seemingly random, senseless reliving of the past" to a more meaningful controllable portion of one's biographical narrative' (1994: 370).

Affect modulation and tolerance

In addition to post-traumatic symptomatology, clients often experience intense affect, including anxiety, fear, depression, shame, hopelessness, and rage. When they begin to focus on their traumatic experiences, these feelings may intensify. One survivor in the incest healing study (Draucker, 1992b) discussed her response when she first began to connect her current experiences with her childhood abuse:

> It was really scary in one sense because my feelings became real and I wasn't – I couldn't sleep – I couldn't stay by myself and it was like the worst thing, of going into therapy or counselling. Everything just became so real. And it became such a controlling force in my life at that time.

Counselling interventions for such affective responses include helping the client to identify and label his or her feelings, to understand the relationship between these feelings and the trauma that they experienced, and to experience feelings without evaluating or rejecting them. In this phase of counselling, clients often need to learn to express feelings verbally or through other means, such as writing, art, and music (Chu, 1998). Counselling interventions at this stage are aimed at the healthy expression of emotion in general, rather than the evocation of trauma-related affect. If clients gain a sense of control over their emotional responses prior to the exploration of abuse, they will be better equipped to tolerate distressing affect when such exploration begins. Additionally, if clients are informed about how emotional responses are related to healing, and are assured of the counsellor's support and availability, they may feel less overwhelmed by their reactions when they begin exploratory work.

Self-injurious behaviours

Clients may present with self-destructive behaviours (e.g. suicide attempts, non-lethal self-mutilation) that may exacerbate as they begin to focus on their sexual abuse experiences. A thorough assessment of suicidal and parasuicidal (self-mutilation) potential may be indicated. Self-destructive behaviours often represent long-standing coping mechanisms in response to overwhelming affect. Self-cutting, for example, may serve to reduce tension or may reflect a sense of self-hate stemming from the abuse (Chu, 1998). Potential for self-harm must be addressed early in treatment; safety planning should be an active, ongoing, and collaborative process (Courtois, 1999). The following counsellor response may be helpful for clients whom the counsellor has assessed as being at risk of suicidal or self-injurious behaviours:

> Working on childhood sexual abuse can be difficult and painful. You've shared with me that at times when you experience painful emotions, you do things to deal with the pain that may be hurtful to you. Therefore, we need to find ways you can keep yourself safe before we start exploring your abuse experience.

Clients and counsellors can devise an action plan specifying what the client will do if he or she becomes at risk for engaging in self-harm. For example, non-suicide contracts detailing actions to be taken in the event of suicidal ideation can be helpful. Action plans may include: self-control techniques (e.g. becoming involved in some activity), calling the counsellor or a hotline, or going to the emergency room of a hospital in the event of imminent danger. Designing such explicit agreements demonstrates the counsellor's concern for the client's safety while giving the client responsibility for his or her actions by devising specific guidelines for managing self-destructive urges. Cognitive-behavioural approaches for dealing with continuing suicidal ideation and self-mutilation, such as those outlined by Meichenbaum (1994), Beck (1994), and Linehan (1993), may be indicated.

Aggression against others

Counsellors may help clients anticipate and prepare for aggressive impulses that might arise when they begin to explore abuse issues. Aggression may be a special concern for male survivors. Bruckner and Johnson (1987), who conduct group therapy with male survivors, reported that group members have often expressed intense anger following disclosure. This anger was sometimes accompanied by plans for retribution, including physical assault on offenders. Counsellors need to assess the potential of harm to others, while validating the client's angry feelings. A helpful counsellor response to a survivor who threatens or implies intent to harm another might be:

> The rage you feel toward [the offender] is understandable given what he did. You have every right to feel anger that intensely. However, I am

concerned that you are considering harming him, which you may later regret. Let's discuss your plans.

Anger management training, in which clients are taught to express anger verbally and constructively, may be indicated for some clients. Meichenbaum (1994) described a stress inoculation training programme for anger control and conflict management that includes: increasing the client's awareness of his or her anger; education regarding the components and function of anger; learning time-out procedures and relaxation and visual coping skills; cognitive restructuring; the use of humour; and skill-building (communication skills, assertiveness training).

Addictions and compulsions

Clients may present with a variety of addictive behaviours, including substance abuse, eating disorders, and sexual compulsivity; these behaviours may also represent long-standing coping mechanisms used to deal with intolerable affect related to earlier trauma and must be addressed prior to exploratory work. Some counsellors may have the training and expertise to deal with such problems in their own practices; others may refer the client to self-help groups, specialized treatment programmes, or practitioners who specialize in these issues. Structured treatment manuals and therapy guidelines that address chemical dependency (Brower et al., 1989; Brown and Fromm, 1986; Meichenbaum, 1994), eating disorders (Friedman and Brownell, 1996; Garner and Garfinkel, 1997), and sexual compulsivity (Schwartz and Masters, 1993) are available.

Sexual abuse survivors may be particularly resistant to involvement in self-help groups such as Alcoholics Anonymous. Several counselling interventions are recommended to deal with this resistance (Skorina and Kovach, 1986). The first step of an AA programme is the admission of powerlessness over alcohol and life, a terrifying prospect for survivors of sexual abuse. Counsellors may discuss the difference between being powerless over a substance and being powerless over one's body or psyche, stressing that admission of powerlessness over a substance is actually a way of gaining control. Because another block to survivors' participation in an AA programme is lack of trust, counsellors can recommend finding home groups and sponsors (i.e., peers from AA with a history of sobriety who provide personal support) who are sensitive to abuse issues. If the survivor is a woman, the choice of an all-female group and a female sponsor may be helpful. Further, the invitation to 'tell one's story' in an

AA meeting may be experienced as intrusive by the survivor; counsellors may help the survivor prepare for this in advance.

Trotter (1995: 100) expressed concern that 'over focusing either on rigid sobriety while ignoring post-trauma symptoms or on issues secondary to serious addiction can create for the recovering person the potential for relapse'. She proposed a developmental model for recovery for the chemically dependent trauma survivor, based in part on Gorski's (1992) recovery-from-addiction model. In the five stages of the model (transition, stabilization, early recovery, middle recovery, and ongoing recovery) issues related to dynamics of trauma, the nature of addiction, and the relationship between trauma and addiction are addressed. For example, during the stabilization phase, the symptoms of postacute withdrawal from alcohol (e.g. inability to think clearly, memory problems, emotional reactions or numbness, sleep disturbances) can mimic the symptoms of PTSD; clinicians are advised, therefore, to refrain from making a psychological diagnosis until the chemical withdrawal is completed. In the model, the 12 steps of Alcoholics Anonymous are interwoven with the stages of trauma recovery. Special attention is paid to relapse prevention by identifying and managing warning signs.

General self-care

Survivors who are not self-destructive in one of the ways discussed above may have a tendency to neglect their general self-care needs (e.g. poor eating habits, neglect of health care, lack of pleasurable activities). This neglect may be due to feelings of low self-worth that stem from the early abuse. One of the participants in the incest healing study (Draucker, 1992b), for example, described how she learned to attend to her personal needs:

> I also learned to do little things that make me feel better about myself, like – really small things but before I go to bed at night maybe I'll fall into bed and I'll think – 'Well, wait, you forgot to brush your teeth and wash your face. Get up and do it!' Whereas before I'd lie in bed and say 'Well, so what?' You'll get a cavity; so maybe your face will break out.

Constructing a self-care plan may be something as simple as agreeing to treat oneself to a desired article of clothing or to take a warm bubble bath after a particularly difficult session; it may be as comprehensive as a nutrition and exercise plan to accompany the counselling process. Clients may need a medical evaluation if they have neglected their health-care needs. Providing for self-care typically becomes easier when survivors are further along in the healing process. Making a commitment to a reasonable plan early in treatment, however, suggests to clients that they can take action to tolerate the painful aspects of the counselling process.

Relationship issues

Clients may present with disturbed interpersonal relationships that must be addressed prior to beginning exploratory work. They may be isolated and without social support, or may be involved in relationships that are stormy and abusive. Courtois stated that: 'Much therapeutic time must be spent identifying and unlearning the "relational rules of abuse and victimization" and replacing them with skills and attitudes necessary for healthy, interdependent connections with supportive others' (1999: 200).

For some clients, social skills training may be indicated so they can begin to seek out sustaining social activities and relationships. Structured educational groups may be useful for this purpose. If the client is currently involved in an abusive relationship, this must be addressed in this phase of counselling.

Because the client may attempt to re-enact old relational patterns with the therapist, the formation of a therapeutic alliance that is mutual and collaborative is necessary. Chu stated, 'The therapy helps to introduce mutuality and collaboration in relationships, rather than control, aggression, abandonment, and betrayal that formed the core experiences of the patient's early life' (1998: 85).

Exploring childhood sexual abuse

The goal of exploratory work

The middle stage of treatment involves exploration of the childhood sexual abuse experience(s). Courtois (1999: 203) stated:

> The primary goal of trauma resolution and integration is for the patient to gradually face and make sense of the abuse/trauma and to experience associated emotions at a pace that is safe, manageable, and not overwhelming.

The solicitation of memories or the intense re-experiencing of early trauma is not the goal of this stage of treatment. As Gold and Brown (1997: 184) argued, 'Neither the clinical nor the research literature on CSA [childhood sexual abuse] and its treatment suggest that *remembering* is the crux or culmination of effective therapy for this population'. The purpose of recounting abuse experiences is to allow for the processing, desensitization, and integration of traumatic memories that return as fragmentary intrusive experiences. Dissociated memories are translated into a coherent narrative. Traumatic material is 'told and retold' until it becomes an integrated aspect of the self and takes on new meaning 'as part of a socially shared autobiographical history' (Brown et al., 1998: 481). According to Brown et al.: 'Recovery of memories is not about gathering information about the past. It is about mastery over what has been unclear or avoided in memory, making meaning out of one's personal history, and achieving integration' (1998: 481).

The emotional expression (e.g. crying) that accompanies exposure to trauma-related material contributes to desensitization (Briere, 1996). The positive emotional experience of the discharge of emotions in the context of a supportive relationship serves to inhibit and counter-condition the fear associated with the trauma. Catharsis pairs the positive experience of emotional discharge with trauma stimuli, thereby counter-conditioning traumatic stress.

The counselling agreement

Counsellors should discuss the rationale for this phase of treatment in terms clients can understand and appreciate. Abuse survivors have often had the experience of describing their experiences to others – only to have them respond with disbelief or excessive interest based on curiosity rather than concern. Clients should, therefore, be active participants in the decision to pursue this phase of treatment, and should explicitly agree to engage in exploratory work.

Pacing exploratory work

The pacing of exploratory work is crucial for therapeutic success. The counsellor should proceed at a pace consistent with the clients' ability to tolerate painful affect. Briere discussed the concept of the therapeutic window, a heuristic used to guide exploratory work. The therapeutic window is:

> that psychological place during treatment wherein appropriate therapeutic interventions are cast. Such interventions are neither so nondemanding as to be useless nor so evocative or powerful that the client's delicate balance between trauma and avoidance is tipped toward the former. (1996: 146)

Counsellors 'undershoot' the therapeutic window if they avoid exploration of childhood trauma or provide only support and validation for clients who have the capacity to engage in exploratory work (Briere, 1996). The trauma is not processed and the client continues to employ avoidance or dissociative defences. On the other hand, interventions that 'overshoot' the therapeutic window are too intense or fast-paced to allow for adequate processing of traumatic material. The client will become overwhelmed with affect and experience increased defensive dissociation. In some instances, counsellors inaccurately label this dissociation as 'resistance'. If the client's defences are not adequate, he or she may become overwhelmed by intrusive symptomatology and resort to soothing, but self-destructive, behaviours, such as self-mutilation or substance abuse. Other clients may flee treatment. Maintaining the therapeutic window, therefore, involves titrating discussion of traumatic material so that clients experience the exposure necessary for desensitization without provoking unwanted avoidance.

Cole and Barney addressed the concept of the therapeutic window, which they believe is characterized by moderate distress and manageable symptomatology. They claimed that the counsellor's task is to 'judge carefully the amount and exposure to . . . memories and affects the survivors can tolerate. That is, the therapist should monitor the "dosage" of intensity and duration so that it is of therapeutically manageable proportions' (1987: 603).

It may be helpful to discuss the concept of the therapeutic window with clients. The counsellor may explain:

> Although painful feelings are necessary for healing, we can discuss the abuse material at a pace that does not feel overwhelming for you. If you feel our discussions are too stressful or emotional to be helpful, we'll slow down. If you start to feel stuck or don't feel anything, we'll begin to explore the abuse in more depth. It's this middle ground where the most productive work gets done.

Once clients understand the concept of the therapeutic window, the counsellor may periodically 'check in' with them to see if they believe they are working within the window.

Working within the therapeutic window requires a balance between interventions of exploration and interventions of consolidation (Briere, 1996). Exploratory interventions involve an examination of traumatic material, both cognitively and affectively. Consolidation interventions focus on safety, support, and stability. Effective therapy requires a balance between these types of intervention, based on the counsellor's ongoing assessment of the client's changing internal state. Clients who are emotionally overwhelmed or functioning poorly will benefit from a greater focus on consolidation; clients who are emotionally stable will profit from a focus on exploration.

Counsellors also need to control the intensity of affect provoked within each session (Briere, 1996). Exploratory work should begin gradually. The intensity of affect should peak in the middle of the session, and time should be left for clients to regain a sense of control and composure before they leave the counsellor's office.

Exploratory work involves a gradual re-exposure to the affect and stimuli associated with traumatic material within the context of a well-established therapeutic relationship. Exploratory work is a form of systematic desensitization in which less upsetting memories are discussed and desensitized before moving on to more painful ones (Briere, 1996). Kluft (1996) recommended processing traumatic material 'from the top down'. The client is asked to describe consciously available material first. Unavailable material will often emerge naturally in the course of these discussions.

Because abuse memories are coded both verbally and through the sensorimotor system, exposure and desensitization must include both of these systems. Factual, verbal memories are generally processed first, as they tend to be less overwhelming than sensory memories (physical sensations and affects). Clients are asked first about 'facts' of the abuse (the who, what, when, where) and later about associated affective and perceptual experiences.

DEALING WITH AFFECT   The constricted affective lives of many survivors can be attributed to defensive processes stemming from the abuse, as well as from growing up in dysfunctional family systems where feelings were not respected. Many survivors will initially appear emotionless when describing their abuse experience (Hall and Lloyd, 1989). When asked, these individuals are often unable to identify or express their feelings.

Male survivors may have special difficulty expressing, naming, and understanding feelings. As Johanek (1988: 112) states, 'Most men with whom we deal have learned to avoid experiencing and displaying emotions at all costs. They tend to describe events and their reactions to those events without using emotional terms'. Men may feel especially threatened when asked to explore their feelings in counselling.

Clients may experience different feelings at varying degrees of intensity when exploring the sexual abuse. Sgroi (1989a), for example, suggested that fear, anger, and perception of loss of control are primary responses that occur when survivors begin to acknowledge the reality of the abuse. Survivors learn that these responses are painful but tolerable. Secondary responses such as guilt, shame, and a sense of damage are subjected to what Sgroi (1989a) refers to as contemporary denial – i.e., the denial of current responses to the abuse experience. Although survivors have acknowledged the reality of the abuse, they minimize its importance in order to block the pain of these secondary responses.

Blake-White and Kline (1985) also differentiated the varied feelings experienced by survivors of childhood sexual abuse. They suggested that feelings of guilt and shame are often acknowledged by survivors spontaneously; anger and sadness are often just under the surface and discussion of these feelings can be facilitated by the counsellor. The stronger emotions of terror, despair, abandonment, fear of pain, and fear of being alone may continue to be denied.

Counsellors should first validate expressed emotions so that survivors can learn to trust and accept their feeling states and then work toward increasing the survivors' awareness of deeper, repressed emotions. There are several interventions that can be used to facilitate this process. First, counsellors may ask clients to name and describe feelings. The following interaction exemplifies a possible counsellor response when a client describes an event, but does not connect it with an affect.

> *Client*: I remember being so all alone. I was only five, for goodness sake. My mother and father were separating so I spent lots of time with him [an abusive babysitter]. I knew I was losing my father, and my mother in some ways too. She was so depressed.
> *Counsellor*: As you describe this experience, what are you feeling?
> *Client*: Sad, incredibly sad. I was only five. I was losing everyone.

When survivors do respond with feeling statements, counsellors can acknowledge the feelings with empathic responses:

> *Client*: The devastation I felt when my mother found out was tremendous. Even now, years later when I see her I want to fall through the floor; I just want to be invisible. I was her perfect angel and I was sleeping with her husband. I would have rather died than let her know what a slut I was.
> *Counsellor*: As a child you experienced great shame. It is a feeling that's stayed with you all these years, still causing you pain.

Third, when working with clients whose families, or society, discouraged the expression of feelings, counsellors may address this dynamic. The following interaction is with a male survivor:

> *Client*: He was my own brother. I looked up to him. When I realized what he did . . . [starts to cry]. See, I'm still a wimp today.

Counsellor: It sounds like you've gotten the message that 'real men don't cry'. That message prevents you from allowing yourself to feel sad about a sad thing that happened to you. Where did that message come from?

Retrieving repressed memories

As mentioned previously, most trauma experts have suggested that repressed memories, or otherwise unavailable material, will emerge gradually throughout the course of treatment as the client's capacities to tolerate painful material increase and defensive dissociation decreases. The use of specialized memory recovery techniques is generally unnecessary.

Brown et al. (1998) argued, however, that there are some cases where memory retrieval techniques may be appropriate: 'Specialized memory recovery techniques are sometimes indicated when . . . the patient is suffering from a more pervasive or extreme amnesia for trauma . . . that has not been reversed by the previous methods designed to minimize memory accuracy errors, such as free narrative recall' (1998: 483–4).

These authors recommended that if it is necessary to use specific interventions to facilitate memory retrieval, a step-wise approach be used. Techniques with the lowest likelihood of causing memory errors, such as free narrative recall, are used first. If these approaches do not reverse the amnesia, techniques that involve a mild increase in memory error rates, such as transference interpretations and context reinstatement combined with free recall (having the client focus on a period of time in which the abuse probably occurred) should be tried. If these are not successful, state-dependent recall techniques (focusing on trauma-associated affect or using techniques to amplify affect), which are associated with a mild to moderate increase in memory error rates, might be considered. A modest increase in memory error rates is associated with specialized memory recovery techniques such as hypnosis or age regression; these techniques should be used with extreme caution only by counsellors who are well trained in their use. A high increase in memory error rates is associated with interrogatory and coercive interviewing, including the supplying of false or misleading information; these methods are always ill-advised.

Mourning

Exploring the abuse experience often provokes a period of grief and mourning as survivors come to terms with the reality of the abuse and the losses and missed opportunities associated with it

(Chu, 1998; Courtois, 1999; Herman, 1992). Survivors may mourn the loss of their childhood; their psychological and, in some cases, physical integrity; and the capacity to trust others:

> The telling of the trauma story thus inevitably plunges the survivor into profound grief. Since so many of the losses are invisible or unrecognized, the customary rituals of mourning provide little consolation. The descent into mourning is at once the most necessary and the most dreaded task of this stage of recovery. (Herman, 1992: 188)

Herman suggested that resistance to mourning may take the form of fantasies of revenge, forgiveness, or compensation. During this time, the survivor may be at increased risk of suicide. Positive memories of caring others in the survivor's life, or the survivor's own capacity for compassion, may serve as 'a lifeline during the descent into mourning' (1992: 194).

Case example

The following case exemplifies the process of exploring an experience of childhood sexual abuse. Susan, a 40-year-old woman, sought counselling because she was distressed about the 'direction' her current relationship with her partner Ray, aged 52, had taken. Susan had dated Ray steadily for four years and had hoped to marry him, but he never proposed. She reported that their sex life was 'OK', although she had always been inorgasmic. Ray was not interested in a 'commitment' such as marriage. He claimed his prior marriage had been 'hell' and he was still supporting his two teenage sons. Susan stated that she had accepted this, but was very upset to learn recently that Ray had been dating another woman.

Susan had worked for 21 years as a secretary and a bookkeeper for a small local industry. She indicated that she did very well at her job, but sometimes felt 'pushed around' by her boss. Describing herself as a 'shrinking violet', she reported that she had only two close female friends. She had little contact with her elderly parents, who lived approximately one and a half hours' drive away.

Susan had never been married but had been in two long-term relationships prior to meeting Ray. She claimed both men were 'losers', both were alcoholic, and one had been physically abusive to her. She reported being very grateful that Ray was 'different' from these men. Susan denied using alcohol or drugs, but she did discuss a significant weight problem and admitted to occasional binging in the past. She had sought counselling on several prior occasions and reported feeling somewhat better about herself after each attempt at counselling. She denied any significant trauma symptomatology, self-destructive behaviour, or anxiety or depression.

During the initial interview, Susan was asked about sexual abuse. She readily revealed that she had been molested by an uncle on several occasions over three summers, from the ages of 9 to 11. Her uncle had a farm that she and her younger brother visited during school vacations. She stated that her uncle had 'taught' her to perform oral intercourse on him and told her she would need to know how to do this to boys when she got older. She reported being 'disgusted' by the experience but preferred the freedom she experienced on the farm to the strict rules (e.g. early bedtime, many 'chores', frequent church attendance) of her parents, who were 'strict fundamentalists'. Susan described her parents, who were neither physically nor sexually abusive, as 'good people' who worked hard but who did not show any emotion.

After one summer when the abuse was particularly bad, she and her brother never returned to the farm and did not have much further contact with this uncle. Susan always wondered if this was because her mother found out what had happened, and recalled being very worried that this was the case. Nothing was ever said, however, about the visits to the farm. Susan stated that she had put the abuse behind her and had forgiven her uncle because he was 'sick'.

Susan had not discussed the sexual abuse in her prior counselling situations because she had not been asked about it. She readily disclosed the abuse on inquiry, but minimized the impact that both the abuse and the family dynamics surrounding the abuse had on her life. The following interaction between Susan and her counsellor illustrates this dynamic:

Counsellor: What was the experience with your uncle like for you?

Susan: I felt like a tramp, sort of. Mostly I hoped my mother would not find out. It was so long ago though. He was probably sick. I do not think he meant to hurt me. I'm sure I'm over it. In fact, to be perfectly truthful, I really don't like to talk about it.

Counsellor: Yes, these experiences can be hard to discuss. Initially, talking about them can feel like you are digging up the past for no reason. Could the experiences you had with your uncle and other childhood experiences be related in some way to the concerns you have today?

Susan: Well, my experience with my uncle could I suppose have something to do with my sexual problem, and maybe even with my track record with men. Every so often – actually, quite often – I think about it. But it is Christian to forgive. Maybe I am too forgiving. How many times have I forgiven Ray? Mostly I think I just wanted to have fun on the farm. I could not really be a kid anywhere.

Because Susan was functioning relatively well without significant psychiatric symptomatology, the preparatory phase of counselling was brief. The counsellor did address Susan's history of binging, but Susan felt this was not a current problem. Susan enlisted the support of her closest friend, Connie, as she began to discuss painful issues in counselling. The exploration of the sexual abuse began with the following interaction:

Counsellor: Describing this experience with your uncle helps me to appreciate and understand what you went through as a little girl, and helps you begin to sort through what happened and make sense of it. However, we can go at your pace and stop whenever you feel the need to. Are you feeling ready to start telling me what happened?

Susan: Yes, I am ready. I just do not really know where to begin.

Counsellor: Why don't you start with the first incident you remember.

Susan: I think I was 9 – maybe 10. I had been at the farm only a day. I was really happy to be there. Uncle Bob treated me real nice. He had bought me some new dresses. Anyway, I was in the barn. He came out and told me how pretty I was. No one ever said that to me. Come to think of it, no one does now either. [*Laughs*] Even though I was skinny then I was pretty homely. Anyway, he told me he was going to teach me how to kiss boys as they would be wanting to kiss me because I am pretty. Then he said I needed to learn about petting. That's when he began to fondle my breasts.

Susan began to describe her experiences in great detail and began to remember more invasive sexual activities. Over the next several sessions, she began to recall some sadistic aspects to the abuse (e.g. being tied up, being whipped). After a particularly difficult session, during which Susan described her rage at her mother because Susan was not able to talk to her about the abuse, Susan reported a serious binging episode. Shortly after, she left counselling at Ray's request. He told Susan she need not 'dig up the past'. Repeated phone calls from the counsellor went unanswered.

Four months later, Susan returned to counselling. She informed the counsellor that Ray had left her for another woman and that she had started to think more and more about her relationship with her uncle and her 'poor choice of men'. She had experienced nightmares related to some especially violent episodes. She also reported a dramatic increase in her food consumption, although she denied further binging. She and her counsellor worked on a self-care contract, which included her participation in a Weight Watchers' group, a short daily walk, and a 'no binge' agreement.

They also discussed some techniques she might use to manage her nightmares. At this point, Susan and her counsellor agreed to continue their work on her childhood experiences and to explore the connections between these experiences and her current problems, but at a slower pace.

Susan described more abuse incidents, which had involved progressively more invasive and physically violent sexual activities; techniques used by her uncle to continue to engage Susan in the abuse; her memories of her childhood reactions to the abuse; her relationship with her parents at the time of the abuse; and the circumstances in which the abuse stopped. Although Susan had initially denied being distressed by the abuse experience, she slowly began to describe her feelings in depth. She remembered feeling like a 'dirty girl'. She experienced much guilt because she hated the sexual activity, but enjoyed the attention from her uncle. Mostly, she reported fearing her parents would discover what had happened. She imagined they would completely reject her or bring her 'sins' to the attention of their minister. She experienced terror at being discovered and abandoned. Betrayal, by both her parents and her trusted uncle, emerged as a key issue for her.

With the support of the counsellor, Susan would take frequent breaks from what she called 'heavy stuff'. She would discuss more day-to-day problems before returning to discussion of the abuse and the issues surrounding it. Susan continued to connect her past experiences with her current distress. She recognized that as a child she could not express her needs for attention or protection. She considered herself to be 'bad' and, therefore, not worthy of having either of these needs met. She began to see her choice of men as being related to her belief that she did not deserve better, and her sexual dysfunction as related to her belief that she did not deserve sexual pleasure. After approximately one year of counselling, she began to feel better about herself. She had lost a considerable amount of weight. Her nightmares subsided. She did become involved with a man, Bob, who had been introduced to her by Connie. Bob was 'not always as considerate' as she would like, but was not abusive. She chose not to become sexually intimate with Bob, although he sometimes pressured her for a sexual relationship. Susan decided to stop counselling because, 'I know I have more to work on but I just want to enjoy feeling better for a while'.

Discussion

Abuse-focused work was indicated for Susan as her childhood experiences, both the abuse by her uncle and her parents' lack of emotional support, seemed to be related to her current difficulties, including her problematic relationships with men, her sexual dysfunction, and her self-image. Because the exploration phase began too quickly and intensely, Susan engaged in problematic coping responses and fled from treatment. When she returned, the counsellor addressed Susan's need for stabilization and paid increased attention to her 'therapeutic window'. At a slower pace, Susan was able to share many abuse experiences with her counsellor and addressed multiple family issues that had caused her pain. Memories that had been dissociated were integrated into Susan's narrative. No specialized memory recovery techniques were needed. She was able to connect her current distress with aspects of her abuse history and began to make some desired changes in her life. The counsellor respected Susan's choice to take a break from counselling and invited her to return if she wanted to continue her work at a later point.

5

Reinterpreting the Sexual Abuse
Experience from an Adult Perspective

D escribing sexual abuse experiences allows clients to begin to interpret them from an adult perspective. Because dissociative processes begin at a time when the child's cognitive skills are still developing, survivors retain a 'child's concept of the event' (Blake-White and Kline, 1985: 398). Individuals who were maltreated as children often judge their behaviour by attributing to themselves, as children, the adult resources of freedom of choice, social support, and the power of reasoning. They believe, therefore, that they were to blame for the abuse, enjoyed it, or could have stopped it and did not. These beliefs often remain unchallenged because the survivor has not shared them with others. In many cases, important others in the survivor's life reinforced his or her sense of blame and responsibility. In counselling, survivors may reinterpret their childhood experiences using an adult understanding of their stage of development and the dynamics of their family at the time of the abuse. The issues that are important for survivors to reframe in this way and counselling procedures that can facilitate this are discussed in this chapter.

Issues to reframe from an adult perspective

Attribution of blame

Survivors' self-blame for the abuse is a key therapeutic issue (Chu, 1998; Courtois, 1999). Herman suggested that, for women, self-blame reflects the attitudes of society that blame the daughter, or at times the mother, for sexual abuse that occurs in the family. She described this myth: 'Ensnared by the charms of a small temptress, or driven to her arms by a frigid, unloving wife, Poor Father can hardly help himself, or so his defenders would have us believe' (1981: 36). Herman argued that the concept of the

'Seductive Daughter' is culturally embedded in religious traditions (e.g. the biblical story of Lot and his daughters), popular literature (e.g. the story of Lolita), and even some clinical literature. Westerlund (1983) listed three attitudes of society that contribute to the self-blame of the female survivor: females incite male sexual behaviours; 'boys will be boys'; and it is the responsibility of females to control male sexuality. One participant in the incest healing study (Draucker, 1992b) stated:

> Your parents teach you that you are responsible if you get pregnant or if you have sex with a boy. You are the one that's responsible, you're the one that's in control of the situation and, you know, if your dad's taking advantage of you, you are responsible.

Offenders often tell child victims that they are to blame for the abuse. Children may also receive blaming messages from significant others; many survivors believe the sexual abuse was punishment for being 'naughty'. Undoubtedly, incestuous family dynamics, as outlined by Gelinas (1983), also reinforces self-blame. Due to the process of parentification, incest survivors learn to assume responsibility for the feelings, needs, and behaviours of others.

Male survivors often blame themselves for failing to protect themselves against the offender (Draucker and Petrovic, 1996, 1997; Struve, 1990). This may result in internalized anger or compensatory behaviours to regain control (e.g. aggression, exaggerated masculine behaviours). Boys are taught that males are not victims and should be powerful enough to protect themselves from the intrusion and aggression of others.

Reframing the attribution of blame from an adult perspective entails acceptance of the fact that the offender, not the survivor, is always responsible for the abusive sexual activity. This is true regardless of the 'engagement strategies' (e.g. threat, bribery, force, 'brainwashing') employed by the offender (Sgroi and Bunk, 1988). By virtue of their stage of psychosocial and cognitive development and their dependent position within the family structure, children are unable to make a free choice regarding involvement in sexual activity. It is the responsibility of the adult, or the more powerful other, to resist engaging in exploitative sexual activities with the child.

Childhood sexual responsiveness

Because survivors remember experiencing physical pleasure or arousal during the abuse experience, they conclude that they enjoyed and sought the experience. Males, who are often the victims of same-sex abuse, may believe that such responses represent latent homosexual desires (Struve, 1990). Reframing the issue of sexual responsiveness from an adult perspective involves realizing that sensations experienced by children are natural physiological reactions to sexual stimulation. Such responses differ from sexual arousal in adulthood, when mature emotional and cognitive responses determine one's enjoyment of a sexual experience. Arousal in childhood does not indicate that the child either sought out or enjoyed the sexual experience.

Issues of attention and affection

Many survivors enjoyed the attention or affection associated with their abuse, and concluded that as children, they instigated the sexual activity. Given the dysfunctional nature of their family, the attention or affection they received from the offender may well have been the only emotional nurturance they received. Because the abused child's life is often void of caring from others, special attention is frequently used as an engagement strategy (Sgroi and Bunk, 1988). Survivors should consider that the need for attention and affection from a significant adult is basic to all children, and that children will naturally try to meet this need in any ways that are open to them. Children may desire the emotional nurturance that accompanies the abuse, but not the sexual activity.

Why me?

Survivors often believe that they were singled out for abuse because of inherent characteristics they possessed as children. This belief is especially prevalent among those who were the only victim within their family. Some survivors assume they were basically bad or 'naughty', and some assume they were especially 'sexy' – although often in an evil way (Herman, 1981). Reframing the 'why me?' issue from an adult perspective allows survivors to appreciate that they were chosen as victims, not because of any inherent personality defects, but because of factors related to the offender's motives or to the family dynamics. The offender often seeks a child who is parentified, vulnerable, or at an age consistent with the offender's emotional or sexual needs. When survivors consider their 'level of sexual knowledge and awareness before the start of the abuse' (Hall and Lloyd, 1989: 112), they realize they did not have the capacity for sexual seductiveness as a child. Seductive behaviours are not the cause of the abuse; they are typically learned as a result of it.

Having kept the secret

Many survivors experience self-blame because they never told anyone of the abuse and, therefore, did not 'stop' it. This concern is especially salient if the abuse went on for a long time, the child was older when the abuse started, the offender's engagement strategies did not include the use of force, and the child had no role in stopping the abuse. Reframing 'secret keeping' from an adult perspective involves having survivors consider what they believed as children would be the consequences of disclosure (e.g. punishment, family break-up, disbelief by significant others, rejection by the offender). It is also important for survivors to consider that telling others, a proactive behaviour, is outside the behavioural repertoire of some children. Disclosure would also have required the availability of receptive significant others, something many survivors did not have. As one survivor in the incest healing study (Draucker, 1992b) stated:

> Even at the time it never occurred to me to tell anybody. I didn't know who to tell, I didn't know how to tell, I didn't know what the conse-quences of telling would have been, I just wanted it to stop. But it never occurred to me to tell. That given the way I was raised in the household, no, I wouldn't have told. I just wouldn't have. Again, that's me being a normal little kid if you will.

Counselling procedures for reframing

There are several counselling procedures that can facilitate the reinterpretation of the sexual abuse experience from an adult perspective. These procedures include cognitive restructuring, techniques encouraging survivors to view themselves as children at the time of the abuse, and the experiential reinforcement of new beliefs.

Challenging beliefs

A cognitive challenge is a response by a counsellor that disputes the survivor's problematic belief with logical reasoning (Sgroi and Bunk, 1988). Cognitive challenges are exemplified in the following counsellor interventions. The first intervention challenges the belief that a survivor caused the abuse because she was flirtatious.

> Harriet: I think I was a flirt even when I was that young. If I had said something he would have stopped. I do think I must have been at least partly to blame. Why else would I feel like such a slut?
>
> Counsellor: A five-year-old child cannot really flirt as we think of flirting because at that age she does not understand adult sexual behaviours enough to know how to flirt. Also, as a five-year-old child, you could

not be responsible for what happened. You were totally dependent on your father and were unable to say no to his requests. As an adult, it was his responsibility to protect you, not to exploit you to meet his needs.

This next intervention challenges the belief that a survivor enjoyed the abuse because he was sexually stimulated.

Jonathon: When I talked to him [the offender] about it [the abuse], he had a good point. In some ways, it felt good to me, the sex I mean. I mean I knew it was wrong and I was scared, but it felt good. I don't know how to say this – but at times I ended up, you know, responding when he touched my private parts. He's right, I must have liked it somewhat.

Counsellor: The response you felt when your brother touched your genitals was a normal physiological response to stimulation, not an indication that you sought or desired the sexual activity.

Cognitive challenges can also be in the form of questions. The following client–counsellor interaction involves questioning aimed at addressing a survivor's belief that she was responsible for the abuse because she never told anyone that it was occurring.

Mary: The abuse went on for almost four years. I was eight when it first started – but about 12 when it stopped. I was almost a teenager, for heaven's sake. I could have done something, you'd think, to stop it, if I had really wanted to.

Counsellor: What might have you done to stop it?

Mary: Tell him, 'Stop it or I'll tell the rest of the world.'

Counsellor: What might he have done if you had done that?

Mary: Deny it. Everyone would have believed him. Famous attorney that he was. What a joke! Do you know he was president of the Lions Club [a local civics organization]?

Counsellor: As a child you realized that telling him to stop or you would tell others would not have been successful in stopping the abuse?

Mary: Also remember he had a violent temper. I was afraid of him. He would beat us for forgetting to bring in the garbage. What would he do if I blew the whistle?

Counsellor: So you believed that, if you told not only would no one believe you, but you would probably have been beaten. What else do you think you could have done to stop it?

Mary: Telling my mother would have been a joke. She couldn't stop him from beating her. She certainly couldn't stop him from coming on to me. I suppose if I really wanted out, I could have run away.

Counsellor: Where would you have gone?

Mary: Probably to the streets. I'd be a hooker now. Lots of us turn out that way, you know.

Counsellor: So even though the abuse went on for four years, until you were 12, as a kid you had no real options for stopping what was happening to you. If you told, no one would have believed you or you would have been beaten. Your mother was no help and you really had no place to go if you did run away. That's a hard situation for a 12-year-old, isn't it?

Mary: Ya, I guess it is.

Cognitive restructuring

Jehu, Klassen, and Gazan (1986) recommended cognitive restructuring as an approach to address distorted beliefs associated with abuse. The counsellor begins by explaining the process of cognitive restructuring to the client. Cognitive restructuring is based on the principle that beliefs influence feelings; if beliefs are distorted, the resulting feelings can lead to behavioural or emotional problems. Jehu et al. advised giving the client an 'everyday' example of how beliefs lead to feelings that lead to behavioural responses. The counsellor might say:

> If Joe concludes that he was turned down for a job because of basic incompetence, he will feel depressed, and it is unlikely that he will apply for another similar job. If, on the other hand, Joe believes he was turned down due to unusually stiff competition, he will feel mildly discouraged, but is likely to keep trying for other similar positions.

The next stage in cognitive restructuring is assisting clients to identify beliefs, which are often automatic or unconscious, that accompany their distress. Techniques to facilitate this include: reviewing the sequence of events leading to the distressing affect, re-enacting a distressing event in a role play, using relaxation and imagery to re-experience the event, responding to questionnaires that outline distorted beliefs commonly experienced by survivors, and keeping a journal to record one's thoughts.

In the following interaction, the client, a 20-year-old college student named Jane, and the counsellor work on identifying Jane's beliefs that result in depressed feelings whenever she visits her mother. One year prior to this interaction, Jane had told her mother how she was abused by her stepfather as a child.

> *Jane*: Every time I go home I end up feeling awful. This time I cried for two days when I got back. I can't understand why. My mom has been great. She's supported me all the way. If I want to talk about it [the abuse], she will. If I don't, she won't mention it. I know from group that most other mothers are not that great. Why do I feel so sad when we are together?
>
> *Counsellor*: During this visit, when did you notice yourself feeling sad?
>
> *Jane*: I made note of it this time. It was Saturday night. I had a date with a high school boyfriend. When we said goodbye to my mom, she looked sad and lonely. I guess I started to feel bad then. Guilty, somehow.
>
> *Counsellor*: What were you thinking at that point?
>
> *Jane*: That I'm getting better, getting on with my life. She's all alone.

Counsellor: What thoughts did you have about her being alone?
Jane: That if I had not brought this all up, she would not be alone now.
Counsellor: The sadness results from your belief that your mom, whom you care about, is lonely. The guilt, and probably the depression you feel when you go home, results from the belief that you are responsible for that.
Jane: Yes, I guess I do believe that.

Assisting survivors to recognize distortions in their beliefs is the next step in the cognitive restructuring process. Survivors are taught commonly exhibited thought distortions (e.g. all-or-nothing thinking, over-generalization, mislabelling, emotional reasoning) and are assisted in identifying these distortions in their own thought processes. The authors (Jehu et al., 1986) gave as an example the negative belief that one was responsible for sexual abuse in childhood because it lasted a long time and was perpetrated without the use of force. They suggested that this belief is due to the common cognitive distortions of personalization (assuming responsibility for events for which one is not to blame) and arbitrary inference (drawing negative conclusions not supported by facts).

The next stage, exploring alternatives, involves assisting the client in replacing distorted beliefs with more accurate, realistic beliefs. This procedure can involve providing factual information (e.g. statistics on the prevalence of childhood sexual abuse, discussion of the dynamics of the incestuous family), encouraging analysis of evidence that supports or disproves the client's conclusions, shifting from the subjective to the objective perspective (e.g. asking the client to judge other survivors in their position), and assisting clients with the process of reattribution of responsibility for the abuse. Alternatives to the belief that one was responsible for the abuse because it lasted a long time would include the following beliefs: the survivor was indoctrinated to please adults, he or she needed the offender's attention, and telling others might lead to being disbelieved, ignored, or punished.

Jane and her counsellor focused on recognizing the distortion in her belief that she caused her mother to be lonely and on exploring alternative beliefs by 'analysing evidence'. After reading a list of the common distortions, Jane decided that her belief distortions included personalization and arbitrary inference. The following interaction involved a discussion of this.

Jane: I assumed my mother left my stepfather because of what I told her. When I read about 'arbitrary inference' I thought that might be applicable because I really do not know why she left him. We have never talked about that.

Counsellor: What evidence do you have that your disclosure was the reason for their separation?

Jane: Timing. It happened shortly, well about six months, after I told her. Why else?

Counsellor: Let's discuss the 'why else?' Are there other reasons why they may have separated?

Jane: Well, they really never got along. He was always away on business. She always stuck with him, though. She thought to leave him would make her a two-time loser. She never got over that my dad left her.

Counsellor: So leaving him was something she considered before your disclosure . . .

Jane: Yes, but she never did it. So I still have to think . . .

Counsellor: What might be some other possible reasons for her leaving him?

Jane: There must be others, I know. I just assumed it was me. You know, maybe I can ask her.

Jane did ask her mother why she had left her husband. Her mother revealed that Jane's disclosure had precipitated her action, but reassured Jane that it did not cause it. Jane's stepfather had been having a relationship with another woman; Jane's mother had known about this for several years. The 'other woman' had a five-year-old daughter. Jane's mother left her husband and then told this woman of her husband's abuse of Jane in order to protect the little girl. Jane's mother had done this with the support of her own therapist, with whom she had been working since Jane's disclosure. She did not tell Jane about the other woman because she believed Jane had 'been through enough'. Jane's mother was lonely, but felt she had taken a healthy step in leaving her husband.

For Jane, cognitive restructuring involved identifying the belief that led to her depressed feelings whenever she came home from college, determining the distortion in the belief, and challenging the belief by considering possible alternatives with her counsellor and by actually 'analysing the evidence' when talking with her mother. Jane was thus able to see that the separation was not caused by her disclosure *per se*, and that what she considered a negative experience in her mother's life was actually a positive, although painful, event.

Dealing with guilt

Sgroi and Bunk (1988) have pointed out that survivors' feelings of guilt are often resistant to cognitive challenges. They reported that while survivors may feel less ashamed about their role in the abuse situation in response to cognitive challenges, they continue to experience significant guilt. For these survivors, guilt may serve a protective function, preventing them from being overwhelmed by feelings of powerlessness. The assumption that the abuse occurred because they wanted it in some way may be less aversive initially than accepting that the abuse was completely out of their control. Being told by a counsellor that they are not to blame and 'should not feel guilty', therefore, can result in overwhelming anxiety. Counsellors can acknowledge the guilt and suggest that such recalcitrant feelings will begin to subside when survivors begin to feel better. This reinforces the idea that the survivors' feelings are under their control and can be abandoned only when they no longer need them (Sgroi and Bunk, 1988).

Sgroi and Bunk discussed a therapeutic technique to address the guilt experienced by survivors. In a survivor group, members are asked to list everything they have done since the beginning of their abuse about which they feel guilty. The survivors and the counsellor (or group therapy members) discuss which of those items constitute legitimate guilt (i.e., what most people would feel guilty about) and which constitute inappropriate guilt (i.e., what most people would not feel guilty about). Hurting a sibling at the time of the abuse would result in legitimate guilt; accepting responsibility for the break-up of the family following disclosure would result in inappropriate guilt. This activity helps survivors to identify specific aspects of their guilt rather than experiencing it as a pervasive, consuming affect, and allows them to receive feedback from others regarding the causes of their guilt. Often, survivors plan expiatory actions (e.g. asking for forgiveness, apologizing) for behaviours that have resulted in legitimate guilt. They also experience a gradual lessening of inappropriate guilt related to the sexual abuse experience.

Respecting survivors' loyalty to their families

Gelinas (1983) discussed another issue to consider in facilitating the reattribution of blame – the need for the counsellor to respect survivors' loyalty to their family of origin, including the offender. Survivors may continue to feel protective, and in some cases loving, toward those who were responsible for their abuse or to other family members who were present when the abuse occurred. If family loyalties are ignored by counsellors who prematurely encourage the expression of anger, survivors' resistance to the reattribution process will increase. Survivors must have the opportunity to express their positive feelings toward the offender and the family. If these feelings are accepted by the counsellor, survivors can then explore issues of responsibility without feeling the need to defend family members.

Encouraging survivors to see themselves as children at the time of the abuse

Many of the cognitive procedures discussed above can be reinforced by the use of techniques that allow the client to consider more experientially their 'childlikeness' at the time of the abuse. Hall and Lloyd refer to this process as 're-entering the world of the child' (1989: 169).

Viewing photographs of themselves at the time of the abuse and discussing their reactions to the photographs with a counsellor or in a group setting can reinforce survivors' perception that as children they were incapable of initiating or consenting to sexual activity (Cole and Barney, 1987; Hall and Lloyd, 1989). Family photographs allow clients to experience visually how small and dependent they were, and how large and powerful the offender was. Survivors can then often sympathize with the child in the photo, something they were unable to do for themselves as children.

Another technique that can serve a similar purpose is having survivors observe children who are close to the age they were at the time of the abuse (Gordy, 1983). Visiting a nursery school class, for example, can be a powerful experience for survivors, enabling them to get in touch with their childhood needs and limitations. Some clinicians (Gordy, 1983) have suggested supplementing such activities with discussion of the stages of normal growth and development (e.g. Erikson, 1968) to help survivors understand how the abuse interrupted their emotional growth as children.

Reinforcing reattribution of responsibility with other survivors

Bibliotherapy

Contact with other survivors is a way of reinforcing reattribution of blame. Learning how other survivors were engaged in the abuse, why they maintained their secret, and how they dealt with issues of responsibility can help clients more easily come to accept that they were not responsible for their own abuse. One way of learning about the experiences of other survivors is by reading about their lives. This can initially be less threatening than speaking personally with other survivors and is often done by survivors prior to entering group counselling. Books written about incest experiences include: *Daddy's girl* by Allen (1980); *I know why the caged bird sings* by Angelou (1971); *Kiss daddy goodnight* by Armstrong (1978); *I never told anyone: Writings by women survivors of child sexual abuse*, edited by Bass and Thornton (1983); *Father's days* by Brady (1979); *Voices in the night: Women speaking about incest*, edited by McNaron and Morgan (1982); *Inside scars* by Sisk and Hoffman (1987); and *Men surviving incest* by Thomas (1989).

Group counselling

Involvement in groups with other survivors of childhood sexual abuse is another powerful way to reinforce new perceptions. In groups, survivors often find that the engagement and secrecy strategies used by their offenders and family were similar to those used in other families. Gordy (1983) reported that members in her group identified a 'central motif', which was that offenders frequently used brainwashing (e.g. convincing the child she had solicited the abuse) as a method of ensuring the child's silence and continued participation in the sexual abuse activities.

Discussing issues of responsibility, engagement processes, 'why me?' issues, and secret keeping within the group setting can be especially useful. Survivors find they can appreciate the fact that their peers were not to blame, had reasons for keeping the secret, and were powerless to stop the abuse. Because it is easier to be 'objective' when evaluating the abuse situations of others, this process can reinforce survivors' developing beliefs about their own abuse.

Reaffirming new beliefs

Reframing the abuse experience, especially the reattribution of blame, can be reinforced with techniques involving vicarious or actual encounters with the offender or with significant others. These techniques include role playing, letter writing, and planned confrontations.

Role playing

After survivors have worked on reframing the abuse emotionally and cognitively from an adult perspective, it is helpful if they can assert their new beliefs experientially. When the survivor can vicariously verbalize a new belief to the offender or to important others, it can serve both to reaffirm the belief and to further integrate the affect associated with the belief. Role playing may be done by using the Gestalt empty-chair technique, in which the survivor is asked to imagine the offender or other person sitting before them. They can prepare a statement summarizing their new beliefs or discoveries, their feelings associated with these discoveries, and any questions they may have for the other individual before carrying out the role play. It is important for survivors to process their feelings and reactions to this experience as the role playing can be very powerful. Examples of role play scenarios may include:

- a female survivor telling her father that she now realizes that as a five-year-old child she was too young to initiate the abuse. Therefore, she was not a 'seductive little thing,' as he had always called her;
- a male survivor telling his uncle, the perpetrator, that although he did experience sexual arousal during the abusive experiences, he did not enjoy or seek the sexual activity. The survivor expresses his anger toward the offender, reaffirms his sexual preference, and then tells his uncle that he (the survivor) no longer needs to hide his feelings behind a 'macho' image;
- a female survivor listing to her mother all the reasons she kept the abuse by her father secret for so many years. She expresses disappointment that her mother was not perceptive enough to see, or strong enough to admit, that the abuse was occurring.

The following client–counsellor interaction demonstrates how the counsellor may facilitate the role play described in the first example. An empty chair faces the client, Brenda. She has imagined that her father, whom she has not seen for many years, is in the chair. Brenda has made a list of things she would like to cover and has given this list to the counsellor to help prompt her.

Counsellor: What would you like to tell your father?

Brenda: What a jerk he is.

Counsellor: Why don't you tell him directly.

Brenda: OK, I think what you did to me when I was a little girl was horrible. It hurt me terribly. In fact, it really affected the rest of my life.

Counsellor: Would you like to tell him how it hurt you?

Brenda: Yes. I grew up thinking I was to blame. You told me it happened because I was seductive. It started when I was only five years old. Ever since then I've thought all I was good for was sex. I thought I was not good enough to have anyone love me.

Counsellor: I know you also wanted to tell your dad what the abuse was like for you when you were little.

Brenda: I was frightened to death. It hurt so much at first. I used to pretend I wasn't there, like it was a dream. Once Mom took me to the doctor for an infection. I felt so dirty. For years after I grew up I could never go to the doctor. I've had so many medical problems. Back then I prayed I would die. That's what you did to your little five-year-old girl. [*Starts to cry*]

Counsellor: You look at what happened differently now than you used to. Tell your father what you've come to believe.

Brenda: I now believe that it was not my fault. It was entirely your fault. You betrayed me. I did not know enough to be seductive at first. I learned that from you and then that was the only way I knew how to be with men. Now, I know I can be loved for me, as a person, not because I'm 'sexy'. That was a line you fed me to keep me involved with you.

Counsellor: What else would you like to say to your father now?

Brenda: I don't wish you harm but neither do I forgive you. Mostly I want you to know what you have done to me. You'll have to live with that.

The counsellor asked Brenda to take a few minutes at the end of the role play to gather her thoughts. She and the counsellor then discussed what the experience was like for her. Brenda stated that she began to feel very sad when discussing how she had felt as a five-year-old. At this point in the role play, she re-experienced the helplessness she had remembered from childhood. By telling her father her new beliefs, she was able to feel a sense of control. After the role play, Brenda identified her main feeling as sadness over the loss of her childhood, which her father had taken from her. The role play helped her to reinforce the conviction that the abuse was not her fault.

Letter writing

A similar technique to reaffirm new beliefs is the use of the unsent letter (Faria and Belohlavek, 1984; Hall and Lloyd, 1989; Joy, 1987). Survivors write a letter to the offender or to others with whom they wish to share their new beliefs regarding the abuse. This technique is effective for survivors who find the empty-chair technique too threatening or for survivors who find its dramatic aspects too awkward. The letter remains unsent, as this allows survivors to express their thoughts and feelings without concern for the other's reaction. As with the role play, it is important that the counsellor process the experience with survivors by exploring what it was like for them to write the letter and what feelings were associated with the experience. (Actually mailing the letter involves issues similar to confrontation, which is discussed below.) Survivors may wish to keep the letter in a safe place and add to it as they continue to develop new beliefs or experience new feelings.

Confrontation

Confronting the perpetrator can be a powerful opportunity for survivors to assert their new beliefs and perceptions of the abuse experience. Because confronting the perpetrator has many ramifications for the healing process of survivors, it should be discussed thoroughly in counselling before the confrontation occurs (Agosta and Loring, 1988; Hall and Lloyd, 1989; Swanson and Biaggio, 1985).

Agosta and Loring (1988) have stressed that the decision to confront the perpetrator must originate with survivors themselves, since it is imperative that the confrontation be their choice. It is also important for survivors to realize that a confrontation with the offender is not a prerequisite to healing; rather, it is an experience that can be very beneficial for some survivors. Confrontation is most successful when survivors use it to assert, rather than to test out, their new insights related to the sexual abuse. If survivors continue to struggle with denial, minimization, or self-blame, they are not ready to confront the offender, as the offender's response of denial, minimization, or blaming the survivor could be detrimental to the survivors' healing (Hall and Lloyd, 1989). Many survivors may harbour the hope, even without realizing it, that the offender will admit to the abuse, fully recognize the impact it has had, and ask for forgiveness. If survivors can verbalize this hope, they often realize it is unrealistic and re-evaluate their need for the confrontation.

It is also helpful for clients to consider what feelings the confrontation experience might provoke. Because a confrontation can evoke strong affective responses and at times a return of trauma symptomatology, survivors may need to provide for their self-care, safety, and self-nurturance.

One participant in the incest healing study (Draucker, 1992b) gives an example of an unplanned, unsuccessful confrontation with her brother during a family reunion:

Out of the blue I just said, 'Do you remember when we were eight – or when I was eight and you were eleven', and described the first incident of incest. He's like 'Well, yeah, you know. I think I remember that.' And the way he was talking about it, it was like someone else had done it, not himself . . . and I kept asking more and more questions – just to verify that yes, at least it happened and I'm not crazy, you know, it did happen. And then I said, 'How do you feel about that?' and he said, 'I don't feel responsible. My hormones were going crazy on me during adolescence and I had no control. I didn't know what I was doing.' . . . I said, 'I want you to say you're sorry.' He said, 'No, I'm not going to say I'm sorry because it's not my fault. I couldn't help myself.' And that was the end of that confrontation and that plummeted me down because

OK, he's not going to take the blame for it, then it must have been my fault. So I took the blame and hated myself. So all last year I was really hating myself. That's what led to my intense misery.

In addition to an awareness of the emotional risks of a confrontation to the survivor, counsellors, due in large part to the false memory controversy, have become increasingly sensitive to issues of harm to third parties. Courtois stressed that counsellors should not advise any action with the potential to harm others, such as confrontation, but should explore the advantages and disadvantages of such actions:

I require as a condition of treatment that patients not make an impulsive and/or unplanned disclosure of abuse (whether known or suspected), especially to the alleged perpetrator or other family members. Any decisions to confront or disclose the abuse must be carefully discussed, decided upon, and planned, since it carries considerable risk potential to both the practitioner and the patient. If a patient does not abide by this agreement, I reserve the right to discontinue treatment and make a referral. (1999: 173)

Brown et al. express similar cautions:

If a patient does decide to confront an alleged abuser, it is critically important for the therapist to clarify in writing that the confrontation does not create any type of therapeutic relationship between the therapist and alleged abuser. This should take the form of a written release by the patient that acknowledges that the confrontation may be emotionally distressing to both the alleged abuser and the patient. Informed consent documents should not be signed by the alleged abuser because that would create an appearance of a professional relationship. (1998: 503)

Counsellors may assist the client to prepare for a confrontation if he or she continues to express the desire for this after carefully considering all ramifications; has progressed significantly with issues of denial, minimization, and self-blame; and is not motivated by hope of the offender's contrition. Clients must first decide how they would like to confront the offender (face to face, over the phone, by sending a letter). The pros and cons of each of these approaches should be discussed. Sending a letter may be less threatening, but may leave the survivor wondering whether the letter was received and what the offender's response was. It is, nonetheless, often the method used when the survivor and the offender have been estranged for some time and the survivor does not desire personal contact. Confrontation over the phone can be less threatening than a face-to-face confrontation and is safer if violence by the offender is a concern. However, the survivor is not privy to the offender's non-verbal responses and the offender can easily choose to hang up the phone at any time.

The same survivor discussed above described a more successful confrontation with her brother approximately a year after she had been in treatment:

> I was finally able to say, 'You screwed me up – it's your fault.' And that was a big deal for me to say. And I said, 'Consequently, I don't want you touching me ever, ever again. I don't want you to hug me when I come home. I don't want you to kiss me. I don't want to be your sister any more. I'm not hanging out with you any more. Stay out of my way. I am going to get help because I like myself and I'm worth it . . . You're the scumbag that did this to me and I'm going to reverse it if it takes the rest of my life. But you're not going to beat me.' I go, 'I'm surviving. I'm a survivor.' And he was crying, which was a big deal . . . I don't care and I – it was a way of expressing myself and not really giving a s— what he had to say.

Case example

The following case exemplifies the process of reframing an experience of childhood sexual abuse from an adult perspective.

Eleanor was a 42-year-old successful businesswoman who sought counselling to deal with her experience of childhood sexual abuse after she had viewed a TV movie that dealt with incest. From the ages of 8 to 13 she had been abused by her grandfather, who lived in her family's home. The abuse involved sexual fondling that usually occurred when Eleanor would come home from school and her parents were still at work. Although Eleanor described her adulthood as 'fairly normal', the movie caused her to wonder whether her avoidance of any intimate contact with men was related to her experience with her grandfather.

Eleanor made rapid progress in the early stages of counselling. She readily disclosed the abuse to her counsellor and was able to describe the experience in detail. However, after approximately six months in counselling, Eleanor described feeling 'stuck' and wondered whether she should discontinue treatment. When she introduced this concern, her counsellor asked her what she hoped would happen next in the healing process. Eleanor discussed her belief that she was the cause of the abuse, that her grandfather was really just a 'lonely, pathetic man', and that most of the fondling occurred because she would 'snuggle' next to him on the couch while they watched their afternoon TV shows. She claimed that she had hoped that counselling would decrease her feelings of guilt. The more she discussed her experiences, however, the more she realized she wanted and sought her grandfather's attention. The following interaction was aimed at reframing Eleanor's beliefs related to responsibility for the abuse:

Eleanor: I remember feeling miserable all day in school. I was lonely, didn't fit in with the other kids. Actually, I looked forward to coming home to be with Grandpa. He waited for me. I know this sounds stupid, but he always had milk and homemade cookies for me. We would have our afternoon shows. I would 'snuggle' with him on the couch and I liked that, so how can I say he abused me? I really did seek him out. He was just a poor old man. I cannot blame him for what happened. If I had been out playing like normal kids, none of this would have happened.

Counsellor: Tell me more about the loneliness you felt as an eight-year-old.

Eleanor: Well, up until that time we moved a lot. My father did a residency in Chicago; then my mother did hers in Boston. Then back to Chicago, where my father did some research. You get the picture . . . . Anyway, I was never in one place very long and my parents were always at the hospital or the lab. I spent a lot of time with relatives. I think my mother really resented Grandpa's needing to move in with us, because now she had two of us to take care of. I think she regretted having me. I interfered with her work, you know. No, I shouldn't say this. They were OK parents. Now my mother is kind of famous. She was just sort of cold and distant. I never remember either of them playing with me. It didn't help that I was so shy. I guess it's natural that Grandpa and I hooked up. God, I sound like a whiner, don't I?

Counsellor: No. You sound like someone describing a childhood during which you were uprooted a lot, you didn't feel wanted or attended to, and you experienced a lot of loneliness. You were missing the attention and the affection you needed. When your grandfather came along and provided those things for you, that naturally felt good.

Eleanor: Yes, it did feel good.

Counsellor: It sounds like, at that time in your life, your grandfather was the only one available to provide those things. All eight-year-olds need attention and affection.

Eleanor: Yes, so do forty-somethings. [*Laughs*]

Counsellor: How true!

Eleanor: Attention and affection were certainly things my parents did not provide. They gave me everything else. Everything else materialistic, that is. But I knew that the sex came along with the attention from my grandfather. I always knew that.

Counsellor: It sounds like you were needing your grandfather's attention and his affection when you 'sought him out'. Because you could not get those things from others in your life, you sought them from the only adult who was available. It was natural for you to do this as a child. Any lonely eight-year-old would have done the same thing. Seeking attention and affection is very different than seeking, or being responsible for, sexual abuse.

Eleanor: Yes, I guess I really did need him for those other things.

Counsellor: As a child, everything probably seemed confusing to you. Although you needed your grandfather's affection, he also used you sexually. As an adult, you can appreciate that you were naturally seeking to meet your needs for attention and affection; you were not seeking the sexual abuse nor were you responsible for it.

Eleanor: Yes, that is true. The sex part I hated.

In this interaction, the counsellor explored with Eleanor what she had needed as an eight-year-old child and challenged the belief that because Eleanor was desperate for her grandfather's affection, she also desired, and was therefore responsible for, the sexual abuse. The counsellor and Eleanor had several similar interactions to reinforce this belief as Eleanor had been convinced for many years that she had sought the sexual activity.

Eleanor was able to express anger and disappointment toward her 'absentee parents'. Actually attributing the blame for the abuse to her grandfather was very difficult and occurred only after the counsellor encouraged Eleanor to discuss the positive memories she had of him. When she could acknowledge that her grandfather was not a 'horrible monster', she could also acknowledge that he engaged in the sexual activity to meet his own needs. Eleanor struggled for some time before accepting the fact that she could be angry about the abuse without discounting the positive feelings she had toward her grandfather. In the following interaction between Eleanor and the counsellor, Eleanor began to accept her grandfather's responsibility for the abuse.

Eleanor: He was really sweet and kind in many ways. Why he did what he did I will never know. He must not have known how much it hurt me.

Counsellor: As children, we usually assume that adults are all good or all bad. Because your grandfather was kind and attentive, and because you really appreciated much of your time together, you assumed he was all good. Unfortunately, that led you to believe you were bad. As adults, we can appreciate that people have good and bad points and do good and bad things. Your grandfather is no exception. He was kind and gentle and attentive and he also used you as a little girl to meet his own needs.

Eleanor: Yes, he did do that. And because of that I do feel betrayed by him. If he was sick, he should have gotten help. What he did has caused me grief my whole life. Sometimes I do feel angry about that. Yet, I still miss him. That does not make sense.

Counsellor: Maybe it does. You loved him and would naturally miss him. But you can also feel angry and betrayed as well.

Eleanor also struggled with the fact that the abuse had lasted for a long time, past when she 'should have known better'. By considering her emotionally unmet needs, she was able to state that she needed attention and affection as much at the age of 13 as she did when she was eight. Eleanor was quite clear that she did not tell her parents of the abuse because they would have 'kicked' her grandfather out of the house, a prospect she could not tolerate.

Although she decided not to disclose the abuse to her parents, Eleanor identified the need to get some 'closure' on her relationship with her grandfather, who was now dead. She visited his grave, which was in another state, and told him how she had been hurt by the abuse. She explained to him that she could not forgive him, but that she was grateful for the non-sexual activities they had shared and for the attention he gave her. She told him that her sense of betrayal, rather than anger, was now paramount.

There were several aspects of Eleanor's abuse experience that made the reframing process challenging. Reattribution of blame was especially difficult because her grandfather had been her main source of emotional support as a child. For this reason, it was especially important that the counsellor respected the loyalty that Eleanor felt toward her grandfather. Because she did not need to defend him, Eleanor could hold her grandfather, rather than herself, responsible for the abuse. A key issue that Eleanor needed to explore was the emotional void she experienced as a child. She could then see that although she would seek out her grandfather, it was because she craved his affection, a basic childhood need, not the sexual activity. Exploring what an average eight-year-old would know about sex might have further reinforced Eleanor's understanding that her needs were emotional, not sexual. She might also have realized that, as a child, she would have had trouble differentiating affectionate touches from sexual touches.

Although Eleanor responded well to cognitive challenges, the experiential part of her healing seemed to come when she visited her grandfather's grave. The counsellor's role in this was to assist Eleanor in planning what she wanted to say, in anticipating what her emotional response might be, and in planning ways to care for herself following the experience. Eleanor had several debriefing sessions with the counsellor following the graveside visit.

6

Addressing the Context of the Sexual Abuse

B ecause sexual abuse often occurs in the context of disturbed family functioning, exploration of other relevant issues that had an impact on childhood development can be important. This chapter will address the processes of exploring the context of the abuse, especially issues related to the client's family of origin. Such exploration can enhance the ongoing connection of developmental influences with current concerns.

Exploring the context of the abuse

Although focusing on the sexual abuse experience is important, it is essential to acknowledge that sexual abuse occurs within a larger context, often within a family system. Other significant factors that had an impact on the client's development, i.e., 'life context of the sexual abuse' (Sgroi and Bunk, 1988: 148), need to be addressed and explored. Addressing other experiences and relationships, both positive and negative, avoids the suggestion that the client's development was shaped entirely by abuse. As Davis has stated:

> For some survivors it [the sexual abuse] is by far the most pervasive influence. For others, growing up in a racist society, being adopted, living in poverty, or being the first child of five had an equal or greater impact. In assessing its effects on your life, it's important to put the abuse in perspective with the other forces that shaped you. (1990: 138–9)

One survivor in the incest healing study (Draucker, 1992b) stressed the importance of dealing with other contextual issues:

> I think what the incest survivors' group did for me was have a . . . it was a forum for all of us to explore whatever those childhood issues were. It wasn't just the incest, but as soon as I say that, for me what comes up are the abandonment issues.

Significant childhood influences are, of course, numerous and varied. Important factors to explore include family composition (e.g. the loss of a parent through divorce, death, separation; the role of other significant caretakers; the survivor's birth order; the number of siblings in the family), social factors (e.g. ethnic origin, socioeconomic class, religious influences), other significant family pathology or stressors (e.g. parental alcoholism, emotional or physical abuse, mental illness, criminal behaviour), and extra-familial resources (e.g. relationships with teachers, sports activities, counselling involvement).

Family functioning

Recently, the concept of adult children of dysfunctional families has been applied to individuals from families with diverse problems (e.g. alcoholism, sexual abuse, physical abuse, emotional neglect), as these individuals often struggle with similar concerns. For example, there are significant parallels between Gelinas' (1983) description of the parentified child in the incestuous family and Wegscheider-Cruse's (1985) description of the family hero in the chemically dependent family (a family in which at least one member abuses drugs or alcohol). The family hero is the child who assumes responsibility for other family members and contributes to the family's public presentation of normality through his or her good behaviour and achievements. Both parentified children and family heroes assume adult responsibilities and learn to meet the needs of others while denying their own needs, often losing the opportunity for a normal childhood. Other roles identified by Wegscheider-Cruse (1985) include: the enabler, who supports the behaviour of the chemically dependent person by attempting to help or 'cover' for him or her; the family scapegoat, who draws attention away from the family's problems by getting into trouble (e.g. at school, with the law); the lost child, who quietly withdraws from the family; and the mascot, who draws attention away from the family's problems by providing humour and mischief.

Satir (1988) compared the closed system of 'troubled' families and the open system of 'nurturing' families. In a closed family system, communication is indirect, unclear, and non-specific; rules are inflexible and covert; and self-esteem among members is low. In an open family system, communication is direct, clear, and specific; rules are flexible and overt; and self-esteem among members is high. In a closed system, outside influences are discouraged; in an open system, free exchange with the environment is sought. Closed family systems are dysfunctional because they prohibit the growth potential of their members.

Farmer (1989: 18) has identified eight 'specific interactional elements' that are characteristic of abusive families. These elements are: denial; inconsistency and unpredictability; lack of empathy; lack of clear boundaries; role reversal; a closed family system; incongruent communication; and too much or too little conflict. Farmer has also identified the general effects exhibited by adults who have grown up in abusive families. These include: lack of trust, avoidance of feelings, low self-esteem, a sense of helplessness, and difficulty in relationships.

A concept that has emerged from the literature on adult children of dysfunctional families is that of 'healing the child within' (Whitfield, 1989). Whitfield defined the child within as 'the part of each of us which is ultimately alive, energetic, creative, and fulfilled; it is our Real Self – who we truly are' (1989: 1). Due to certain childhood experiences such as emotional neglect, alcoholism, or abuse, individuals learn to deny their child within. This results in passivity; self criticism; orientation toward others; and inhibition of creativity, spontaneity, and joy in adulthood.

Counselling procedures have been developed on the basis of concept of the child within, sometimes referred to as the inner child. Farmer, for example, discussed techniques for reparenting the inner child using imagery. This involves first releasing one's original parents by recognizing that they are the products of their 'own fragmented, injurious childhoods' (1989: 104) and accepting that one no longer requires anything from one's parents to survive. Creating new internal parents is accomplished by imaging a mother and father who possess the desired parental qualities, such as protectiveness, supportiveness, and sensitivity (i.e., a 'Good Mother' and a 'Good Father'). Finally, adopting one's inner child involves first imaging a time from one's childhood when one was hurt and then imaging a 'Good Mother' or a 'Good Father' showing concern and care for one's needs. Farmer suggests that this activity can teach one to provide nurturance for one's own inner child.

Healing is facilitated if survivors are able to place the sexual abuse experience in the larger perspective of their overall childhood development. For example, counsellors may ask clients to consider Farmer's eight elements of abusive families or the roles of a dysfunctional family as suggested by Wegscheider-Cruse. Clients then reflect on those issues that were salient in their own families of origin. Survivors may then consider how, for example, incongruent communication in their family of origin has had an impact on their current communication patterns or how their role as the family hero continues to be carried out in their present lives. It is also useful if survivors are encouraged to discuss the influence of positive intra-familial and extra-familial childhood experiences on their present development.

Case vignette

The following case vignette highlights the importance of exploring the context of the abuse in order for clients to be able to place their sexual abuse experience in a meaningful context. Heather, a 24-year-old graduate student, had been sexually abused by an uncle on several occasions when she was 12 years old. She had sought counselling originally to deal with frequent nightmares and several phobias (e.g. of being alone in the dark, or of taking showers when alone in her apartment). After focusing on the abuse experience, her symptoms essentially subsided. Yet Heather complained that she still felt that there were pieces of the experience with which she had not come to terms. After several sessions spent exploring what was 'missing', Heather decided to explore more closely the dynamics of her family of origin. She had claimed they were a normal, very close family. Her mother and father had maintained that the abusive uncle was truly a black sheep in an otherwise very respectable extended family. When Heather told her father that the uncle had molested her, her father banned him from any further contact with the family. After exploring her family's responses to the abuse more closely, and identifying some family dysfunction, Heather was better able to understand both her response to the abuse and her ways of coping with problems.

Heather: It was weird. They [her parents] were very supportive. They told me it was not my fault, that I shouldn't worry about it. My father told my uncle never to see me or any of the family again. They even took me on a wonderful trip to help me get over it. In fact, at the time I thought it brought us closer together.

Counsellor: Looking back now, what about that seemed weird?

Heather: Well, I guess that when we got back from the trip no more was said. I mean, they were still supportive. When I would dream about my uncle, my mother would come into my room, get me water, rub my back, generally calm me down. But she would never ask what the dream was about. I assumed she did not want to bring up bad memories.

Counsellor: And what do you think now?

Heather: Well now I realize I needed to talk about it. Also, I guess I wonder why they never brought charges against him or got me any professional help. In those days I guess people did not do that as much. But I still wonder why they didn't. What if he did the same thing to one of my cousins?

Counsellor: What does their response tell you about your family?

Heather: I think that they tried very hard to be the perfect family. We never fought, never got angry at each other. Appearance was important to the outside world. Because of this, I think, the abuse was denied, swept under the rug, maybe. They told me it was not my fault, for which I am really grateful, but we never talked any more about it again. They should have at least told my other uncles and aunts to watch out for their kids. I guess by not acknowledging it to the outside world, we could keep our image of the normal family. But, you know, it was not just the abuse. For example, my mother had breast cancer when I was young and never told anyone, not even me, until years later. She quit her job as a schoolteacher rather than tell anyone she had cancer.

Counsellor: How did your family's way of handling the abuse affect your healing?

Heather: It fed into my denial, I think. Made the abuse seem more unreal. Like it never happened. More importantly, I guess, I learned not to face things myself. Do you know, I've had a lump in my breast for six months and I've not had it checked out.

Exploring her family's functioning, both in response to the abuse and more generally, allowed Heather to gain insight into some of her present experiences. Although the trauma symptomatology did seem to result directly from her abuse, other issues she faced (such as her tendency to avoid problems) were also related to family and developmental influences. Until these issues were addressed, she had felt something was missing from her healing experiences.

Non-offending family members

Another context issue is the role of important non-offending family members. Survivors often struggle with their feelings toward other family members who were present when the abuse occurred but did not protect them. Because abuse often involves adult male offenders, often fathers or stepfathers, and female child victims, the non-offending family member most often addressed in the literature is the mother.

Mothers have often been blamed for the abuse that occurs in the family. In both popular and clinical literature, it has been suggested that the cold, sexually unavailable wife drove her husband to her daughter and at times colluded in the abuse to avoid her own sexual 'responsibilities'. The offender is therefore thought to hold no responsibility for the abuse. In reaction to this sexist attitude, some counsellors have discouraged survivors from exploring their feelings toward their mothers. Herman, for example, critiqued counselling approaches that prohibit 'mother-blaming' by survivors:

> Although fathers and not mothers are entirely to blame, victims must be permitted to express the depth of their anger at both parents. The victim who is not permitted to express her anger at her mother or her tender feelings for her father will not be able to transcend these feelings or to put them in a new perspective. (1981: 200)

In addressing reactions toward the non-offending family member, it is important for both counsellors and survivors to differentiate between responsibility for protecting the child and responsibility for the abuse itself (Hall and Lloyd, 1989). As Gelinas (1983) stated, the abuser is always responsible for the sexual contact, whereas all adult family members are responsible for the incestuous family dynamics. The non-offending family member could be any responsible older person or caretaker in the family when the abuse occurred. Because survivors usually struggle with issues related to a parent or parents who did not protect them, non-offending parents will be the focus of this discussion.

Inevitably, clients question the role of non-offending parents in the abuse. There are several possibilities regarding their role: they had no knowledge of the abuse; they suspected but did not acknowledge the abuse; they knew of the abuse but did not intervene; or they knew of the abuse and condoned it (Hall and Lloyd, 1989). Survivors may never definitely know which role a non-offending parent played. After exploring the possibilities and confronting their own denial and minimization, survivors usually come to some conclusion about this issue.

Some individuals state that it is easier to hate the offender than to be angry at the non-offending parent, whom they may still love and with whom they may have close, current contact. As one survivor in the incest healing study (Draucker, 1992b) stated:

> But my stepfather, I don't care about. I was more hurt by my mom staying with him. I couldn't care less. I don't care if I ever see him again. I just don't like him as a person . . . but my mom hurt me more because I care about her more. Do you see that?

It is important, therefore, for counsellors to encourage survivors to express their feelings about non-offending parents. These feelings may range from disappointment that a parent was not strong enough to recognize the abuse to intense rage because a parent knew of the abuse and either ignored or condoned it.

Hall and Lloyd (1989) have suggested that it can be helpful if survivors explore the reasons for the actions or inactions of non-offending caretakers, and place their behaviour in the larger context of the family dynamics. This should not imply that survivors are not entitled to their angry feelings or that they should forgive the non-offending parent for his or her actions. Instead it may help survivors make sense of their own experience. For example, it could be helpful to understand the non-offending parent's family history, which may have included childhood abuse. Such information provides some explanation for the parent's inactivity and inability to protect the child.

Connecting present concerns with childhood experiences

Addressing abuse context issues will facilitate clients' ability to connect their childhood experiences with their current issues. Making these connections occurs throughout much of counselling. Clients gain insight into how certain responses that once served as a way to survive a harmful environment can now be relinquished in favour of alternative, healthy responses. Counselling involves a delicate balance between exploring childhood issues and addressing current functioning. One participant in the incest healing study (Draucker, 1992b) described this process in her own therapy:

> I think then probably what she [her therapist] did for me, or what we worked on together, was to talk about what had happened and for her to help me see how as a child, you start doing things to cope and to get by. And then what she did was bring it into the present day. It seemed like she had a very good ability to – you know, I would come in and start to talk about some problems that I was having today whether it was with my family or my boss or my husband, and in the next few sessions we would get back into the abuse time period and she would help me see how the way I reacted to that was affecting the way I react to people today.

Often, clients respond to the counsellor as they did to significant individuals from their past. They may expect the counsellor to hurt them through rejection, exploitation, or manipulation and respond to the counsellor with fear, mistrust, rage, or excessive dependency. It is important for clients to be given the opportunity to explore their current reactions to the counsellor in relation to reactions they have toward other significant individuals in their lives. To avoid repeating problematic interactional patterns that clients have experienced previously, counsellors should avoid an authoritarian approach, set clear and realistic limits, and reinforce clients' independence and self-acceptance (Briere and Runtz, 1988).

Case study

The following case shows the importance of addressing the context of a sexual abuse experience in counselling. Jerry was a 36-year-old married male who worked with his father in a small family-owned machine shop. He sought counselling at a community mental health centre because he had a depression that he 'could not shake'. Jerry claimed that he was tired most of the time, could not concentrate on his work, and had lost all sexual desire. Although he claimed his relationship with his wife of eight years had always been good, they were currently experiencing some problems because they could not conceive a child. After years of infertility treatment, they had given up trying. Jerry stated that he was content not to have children, but had problems dealing with his wife's disappointment. He reported that she frequently complained that he was unavailable to her emotionally, and that she felt like she was dealing with this loss alone.

Jerry was the youngest of three children. His older brother Tom, aged 44, was an alcoholic who worked sporadically at the machine shop. His older sister Jean, aged 40, was the office manager at the shop. Jerry stated that she was the one who kept things going. Jean was married with two children. Jerry stated that his father was an alcoholic who nonetheless managed to show up at the shop every day for 35 years. His mother stayed at home and was always 'pretty unhappy'.

When asked about significant childhood events, Jerry reluctantly revealed that at the age of 11 he had been molested in the park on his way home from school by two older boys whom he knew. They asked him to play a 'game' with them that resulted in each of them penetrating Jerry anally. Jerry was upset by the experience and told Tom about it. His brother responded by saying it 'sounded like fun' and then molested Jerry himself. This abuse by Tom, involving anal intercourse, occurred several more times. Tom said that if Jerry told their parents of their activities, he would deny it and would beat Jerry for telling. Tom had been physically violent when the brothers were younger.

The initial focus of counselling was on the abuse experience itself. Jerry dealt with issues of self-blame for not standing up to his brother and the other boys, anger toward Tom, and questions regarding his own sexuality. Much of Jerry's counselling also involved addressing the context of the sexual abuse. Jerry was encouraged by the counsellor to describe his family members, their relationships with each other, and major family events. In the following interaction, the counsellor introduces the idea that the experiences that accompanied the abuse could have had an important impact on Jerry's development.

> *Counsellor:* Jerry, you've worked hard dealing with your abuse experiences and the impact they've had on your life. I also wonder about other things that were occurring in your family at that time.
>
> *Jerry:* I'm not sure what you mean.
>
> *Counsellor:* Many things that children experience, not just abuse, can affect them in adulthood. What was your relationship with your parents like at that time?
>
> *Jerry:* Well, it was not good with my dad. I guess you could say he was a drunk . . .

The family did have many attributes of a dysfunctional family. Jerry's dad was an alcoholic and his mother was apparently chronically depressed. Jerry stated that his father drank 8–10 beers nightly until he passed out, although he never missed work. His mother would often complain about his father's drinking. When his dad's business associates called him in the evening, she would tell them that he was bowling or shopping; in fact, he had usually passed out. Because he would get quite irritable when drinking, she would keep the children quiet so as not to disturb him. Jerry claimed that no one outside of the family ever realized his dad had a drinking problem. His mother was always extremely tired and often tearful.

As a child, Jean did well in school and was actively involved in the family business at a young age. The family was 'shocked' when she got pregnant and married at the age of 16, because she had always been 'so good'. As a child, Tom was always in trouble at school and had several minor scraps with the law for various violations (e.g. petty theft, disturbing the peace). Jerry described Tom as a bully who never obeyed their parents. On the other hand, Jerry described himself as a loner in school who never caused the family any trouble. He stated that his family 'kind of ignored me'. He worked in the machine shop as a boy, but he never enjoyed the work.

In counselling, Jerry did some reading on chemically dependent families and became animated when discussing how classically his family members played the roles he read about. His mother's enabling behaviours were clear. He remarked that Tom was the scapegoat, Jean was the hero, and he was the lost child. Having this understanding of his family helped Jerry accept that he wasn't 'just a loser'. He recognized that his family's poor communication styles and isolation from the community, except through the business, were also characteristics of a dysfunctional family.

Dealing with his feelings toward his parents regarding the sexual abuse was more difficult for Jerry. He stated that he had never thought they knew of the abuse, but had begun to question why this was so. It was only after being in counselling for almost a year that he did begin to express disappointment and anger at his parents' failure to protect him from the abuse. He realized that he never told them of the abuse because he believed they could not have helped him. The following interaction represents Jerry's struggle with this issue.

> *Jerry*: I guess I always knew they [his parents] had problems of their own, but I never thought their problems affected me – or had anything to do with what my brother did to me. But maybe, I don't know, if they had not been messed up. I never told them, though.
> *Counsellor*: Remember yourself as a young boy. What kept you from telling them?
> *Jerry*: Well, I probably knew they couldn't – or wouldn't – do anything to stop Tom. He ran wild. They couldn't control him.
> *Counsellor*: It would have been futile to tell them?
> *Jerry*: Yes. When I talk about them they sound like losers. Now I guess I do wish they did something. Ya, I guess some parents might have done something, or noticed something happening, or found out. I wish mine had. I sure wish they had stopped it. They knew he beat me up and couldn't have cared less. [*Speaks softly, begins to fidget*] It's Tom's doing though, not theirs.
> *Counsellor*: Yes, only Tom is responsible for abusing you, and I know you've expressed the rage and hurt you feel toward him. It seems hard, however, for you to discuss your disappointment that your parents did not take action to stop him somehow.
> *Jerry*: Ya, I'm not sure why.

Jerry was able to connect his current concerns with the abuse situation in several ways. He recognized that he was dealing with the pain of infertility by withdrawing from his wife, much as he had withdrawn from his family as a child to try to avoid pain. Although the couple had been given a diagnosis of idiopathic, or unexplained, infertility, Jerry had attributed the infertility problems to himself. As an adolescent, he had extreme concerns about his sexual identity. He realized that currently, on some level, he thought the infertility reflected his lack of 'manliness'. Just as he blamed himself for not protecting himself from his brother's abuse by concluding he was not a 'man', he blamed himself for the infertility by deciding that, regardless of what the doctors said, he was sterile. This served to reinforce his already poor self-concept.

Jerry's healing involved dealing with the abuse experience and the context within which it occurred. As a result of being the 'lost child' in his dysfunctional family, he felt insignificant and was left without the emotional resources to deal with his current crisis. Although much of Jerry's distress was related to the sexual abuse, general family issues clearly contributed to many of his concerns. Once he addressed these issues, he was free to begin to make changes in his life. These changes will be discussed in the following chapter.

7

Making Desired Life Changes

O nce clients have addressed issues related to the sexual abuse experience and its context and have connected their childhood coping patterns with their current concerns, they often begin to make desired life changes and restructure their lives in ways they find more satisfying. This chapter will address some of the behavioural and lifestyle changes frequently made by survivors. Several experts have referred to this work as late phase treatment because clients, having accomplished the goals of exploratory work, are free to focus on self-development and relationship concerns. Courtois stated:

> The gains achieved over the course of treatment, development of a self less encumbered by traumatic intrusions and effects, and continued development of interpersonal connections are consolidated and built upon in this third phase. (1999: 215)

Three areas of adult adjustment that are often addressed at this point in counselling are self-esteem, interpersonal functioning, and sexual functioning.

Self-esteem

Survivors often struggle with self-esteem concerns throughout the healing process. Although the reframing of the abuse experience (as previously discussed) can be effective in addressing the guilt and shame that underlie the survivors' negative self-image, dealing with self-esteem often remains a salient issue even late in counselling.

Although addressing self-esteem is frequently identified as a counselling goal, it is sometimes approached in an oversimplified manner (e.g. giving a client 'positive feedback'). Peplau proposed a model that can guide the counsellor in addressing self-esteem issues in depth (O'Toole and Welt, 1989). This model suggests that there are three dimensions, or self-views, that comprise one's concept of the self.

The first dimension, the *self-views in awareness*, consists of conscious, familiar, and often articulated self-perceptions. These views reflect the messages about oneself that were heard frequently from significant others in childhood. The *self-views in awareness* of the client with a poor self-image are often that he or she is bad, worthless, or dirty.

The second dimension, the *maybe me self-views*, consists of self-perceptions that are not immediately in one's awareness. One may, however, apply these views to oneself if one's attention is directed toward them. These views reflect messages received only occasionally in childhood. For survivors of abuse, the *maybe me self-views* are often positive qualities that perhaps teachers or some other supportive adults in their lives acknowledged. A *maybe me self-view* of an abuse survivor might be that he or she was a good student and a child of some worth to someone.

The third dimension, the *not me self-views*, consists of self-perceptions that are out of awareness. Because these views are associated with severe anxiety, they are dissociated from the individual's experience. An abuse survivor's *not me self-view* might be that he or she is a worthy, valuable individual who possesses basic personal rights. Although these are positive perceptions, such self-views are at odds with the ways in which individuals with negative self-images are accustomed to perceiving themselves.

Counselling interventions

Survivors often make negative comments about themselves that reflect their low self-esteem and require intervention by counsellors. Peplau cautioned counsellors against challenging these negative self-views in awareness with laudatory comments regarding the client's value or worth in an effort to improve his or her self-esteem (O'Toole and Welt, 1989). Although self-views in awareness are often negative, they are comfortable and expected. Simple compliments regarding positive qualities often reflect clients' not me self-views, which are associated with anxiety; these compliments, therefore, evoke defensiveness. Instead of praising clients, counsellors should first facilitate discussion of ways in which a self-view in awareness was noticed by the client or stated by others. Peplau called this method an investigative approach. Table 7.1 outlines a client statement exemplifying a negative self-view in awareness and non-facilitative and facilitative counsellor responses. Peplau believed that this type of discussion will enable *maybe me* statements to emerge (O'Toole and Welt, 1989). A *maybe me*

Table 7.1 *Interventions for statements reflecting the self-view in awareness*

Client statement:	I am a slut. I'm not worth you helping me.
Non-facilitative counsellor response:	I think you are a worthwhile person and I look forward to helping you.
Facilitative counsellor responses:	1 Tell me who first told you that you were a slut. (Exploring when self-view was said)
	2 When did you first feel worthless? (Exploring when self-view was noticed)
	3 Tell me about a specific time that you felt like a slut. (Exploring when self-view was applied)

Table 7.2 *Interventions for statements reflecting the maybe me self-view*

Client statement:	Well, I guess not everyone thinks of me as a slut just because that's what my stepfather told me I was. The other group members don't seem to see me like that.
Non-facilitative counsellor response:	Yes, they see you for the worthwhile human being you are.
Facilitative counsellor responses:	1 Yes, I've noticed they have commented that you have useful things to say. (Feedback-specific observation)
	2 Yes, I've noticed others in the group do treat you with respect. (Feedback-specific observation)
	3 Tell me about other people who do not consider you a slut. (Exploring when self-view is experienced)

statement is often a tentative or conditional positive self-statement. The counsellor can reinforce this statement with specific observations and have clients describe situations in which they have experienced the maybe me self-view. Table 7.2 outlines a client statement exemplifying a *maybe me self-view* and non-facilitative and facilitative counsellor responses.

Peplau emphasized the need for counsellors to address the anxiety that is likely to be associated with the expression of positive *not me self-views* (O'Toole and Welt, 1989). Clients can be encouraged to describe feelings related to a self-view that is at variance with the self-view to which they are accustomed; they can then begin to consider how this new self-view can be applied. Table 7.3 outlines a client statement exemplifying a *not me self-view* and non-facilitative and facilitative counsellor responses.

Table 7.3   *Interventions for statements reflecting the not me self-view*

Client statement:	I realize now that I am not a slut. I am a worthwhile human being.
Non-facilitative counsellor response:	I'm glad you've realized this. It will make a big difference in your life. I'm very happy for you.
Facilitative counsellor responses:	1 What is it like for you to think of yourself in this new way? (Exploring feelings)
	2 Tell me about a situation in which you have applied (or will apply) this new way of looking at yourself. (Exploring ways to apply this self-view)

Peplau's model, therefore, suggests that constructive, positive self-views emerge only after the more familiar self-views are processed, and only if the anxiety generated by the positive self-view is acknowledged and addressed. Positive self-views often do not emerge until late in counselling.

Interpersonal functioning

As the self-esteem of clients improves, they often begin to make changes in their current relationships. Interpersonal problems of survivors range from social isolation to involvement in relationships that are destructive or abusive. Because sexual abuse involves a disregard for the physical and emotional boundaries of children, typically by a supposedly trustworthy other, establishing boundaries between themselves and others, developing trust, and learning social skills are key relationship issues for survivors.

Counsellors may assist survivors in evaluating their current relationships by exploring how these relationships meet the survivors' needs for intimacy and socialization, and how the relationships enhance or detract from their growth and healing. Making connections between past abuse and current relationship difficulties can be important. Clients often discover, for example, that they are unable to express anger in their current relationships because they learned in childhood that the expression of anger resulted in negative consequences (e.g. a beating, further sexual abuse, rejection).

Establishing boundaries

The healing process for survivors often involves learning to establish personal boundaries. In the abuse situation, survivors were frequently part of an enmeshed family system in which they did not experience a sense of separateness from others. The family or the offender may have given the message that this enmeshment was a 'special closeness'. One survivor in the incest healing study (Draucker, 1992b) stated:

> I began to realize that my relationship with my father specifically wasn't what I wanted it to be or had always pictured it to be. There was a nurturing part of what we shared together and a real closeness. And I started hearing things about Daddy's little girl – red flag. Emotional enmeshment – red flag. You know, things that started sending up all these little signals in me, like, hmm, some of what I always felt was real special about our relationship may have actually been rather sick.

Establishing a way to separate the self from others becomes an important issue. The same participant described this process for herself in adulthood.

> You see, boundary issues in general are something that any incest survivor needs to deal with. Since my boundaries in almost every way were totally violated most of my childhood, you know, even emotionally. How far do I let people go with me . . .?

In order to address such issues, counsellors may ask for a description of situations in which the survivor experiences boundary dilemmas, assist the survivor in relating these current situations to the abuse experience, and support the survivor's attempts at establishing his or her personal boundaries. Counsellor responses to the above statement, for example, might include:

> Tell me about a situation you experienced recently in which your boundaries were threatened. How was that situation similar to (different from) your abuse experience? What did you do in the situation? In what ways would you have liked to have set limits on the other person's behaviour? What would it be like for you to set those limits?

Another participant in the incest healing study (Draucker, 1992b) related the following scenario:

> I went to him [a physician] last year and he was new, he was somebody new that I was just going to. And he pulled his stool very close to me and I felt myself extremely uncomfortable. I mean, I was sweating, I could feel my heart racing and I thought, 'Tell him to get away.' I kept establishing in my mind what I had a right to establish with people – that physical boundary. Something kept – I couldn't say it.

In response to a description of a situation such as this, the counsellor should support the client's desire to protect her physical boundaries. A possible counsellor response might be:

Your physical space is very important, and the doctor invaded that space. I support your idea that you have a right to establish your boundaries. What would you like to have said to the doctor?

Establishing boundaries may include rejecting unwanted sexual or physical contact, setting limits on intrusive or exploitative behaviours, establishing independent interests and becoming involved in activities separate from one's significant other, expressing one's opinions or beliefs, expressing negative feelings, and learning to meet one's own needs in a relationship. In some cases, survivors may choose to end relationships that are dysfunctional, destructive, or abusive. Counselling approaches that facilitate the above processes can include assertiveness training (or other interpersonal skills training), group counselling focusing on interpersonal dynamics, parenting skills training, and family or couples counselling.

Developing trust

For survivors, improving interpersonal relationships involves learning to trust others. The goal for survivors is not to indiscriminately trust all, but to be able to make judgements regarding who in their lives are trustworthy.

This process often begins with the counsellor. Clients may be told that the counsellor does not expect instant trust but will strive to act in a trustworthy manner (Sgroi and Bunk, 1988). For survivors, learning to trust others is often a question of accepting that trust is not an all-or-nothing aspect of a relationship; it is something that is built and maintained over time (Hall and Lloyd, 1989). One cannot evaluate another's trustworthiness by generalizing from one transgression or from one trustworthy act. Counselling can assist survivors in judging the trustworthiness of others by teaching them to objectively evaluate the other's behaviour in different situations and at different times. One participant in the incest healing study (Draucker, 1992b) described this process for herself:

My parents have tried to teach me that you don't need anybody, you shouldn't have friends, and they don't have good friends. And, consequently, they're miserable, so they kind of brainwashed me that way. 'You shouldn't need anybody. You can't trust anybody.' Well, I'm not doing that. I like a lot of people and I've made a lot of new friends this semester . . . I always thought people wouldn't like me so I always stayed away from people. I wouldn't go to parties, wouldn't go out to one of the bars. People liked me, but I've always been so afraid no one would like me. And it's not true. I have people tell me, 'I really like you.

I'm glad I met you. You're nice. You're fun to be with', or 'You're really intelligent.' People get really verbally supportive of me and I really need that.

Learning social skills

For many survivors, reaching out to others involves developing and practising new communication and interpersonal skills. Because sexual abuse often disrupts the child's psychosocial development, he or she may not learn skills necessary to form and maintain satisfying interpersonal relationships in adulthood. These skills may include: appropriate self-disclosure (i.e., letting others know of one's personal self), the ability to express affection and caring to others, and the ability to receive affection and caring from others (Sgroi, 1989a).

Social skills training may be helpful at this stage of treatment (Bolton et al., 1989). This training may involve: an assessment of the individual's strengths and weaknesses, attitudes and beliefs, and patterns of social behaviours; response acquisition activities (e.g. behavioural rehearsal through role playing, modelling); and guided practice in natural settings.

Some programmes focus on specific problem areas. Cloitre (1998), for example, proposed a two-phase treatment model for women who have had multiple experiences of victimization. The first phase focuses on affect and interpersonal regulation; the second phase focuses on the emotional processing of trauma memories. The aim of interpersonal regulation training is to help clients negotiate difficult interpersonal situations that require assertiveness and self-control. The ultimate goal of the training is to decrease interpersonal victimization. Role plays are recommended to help the client identify goals and feelings and express them in words and actions. Interventions for addressing negative self-perceptions and guilt and blame reactions that interfere with healthy interpersonal relationships are included. Gradual transitions to healthier social functioning are planned. Cloitre suggests that 'It is important for the client to experiment with new situations and new people, but this should be done in a way that maximizes success in these ventures: task demands should match the client's abilities and readiness' (1998: 297).

Sexual functioning

Once clients have addressed issues of self-esteem and interpersonal relationships, many choose to address concerns related to their sexuality. The sexuality of survivors is often adversely affected by the childhood sexual abuse experience, during which they could not assert their interests, effect an end to the abuse, or understand what was occurring.

Female survivors and sexuality

Maltz and Holman (1987) suggested that due to sexual socialization, women often develop numerous misconceptions about sexuality and sex roles; these misconceptions are exacerbated by an abuse experience. Misconceptions may include the following: sexual relations should primarily meet the male's needs and desires; the role of the female in sexual activity is to be submissive and dependent; women are the property of men; women must satisfy the male's sexual desires, which are powerful and uncontrollable; and sexual activity is a prerequisite for receiving emotional nurturance.

Three aspects of sexuality are particularly influenced by the experience of childhood sexual abuse (Maltz and Holman, 1987). The first is the pattern of sexual emergence in adolescents or young adults. For abuse survivors, this often involves either sexual withdrawal (e.g. avoidance of dates), due to sexual fears and low self-esteem, or promiscuous or self-destructive sexual activity, due to survivors' needs for attention or attempts to control their sexuality.

The second aspect of sexuality that is influenced by the sexual abuse experience is the choice of a same-sex or opposite-sex partner. Although the relationship between early childhood sexual abuse and sexual preference is unclear, a sexually victimizing experience can undoubtedly influence one's choice of sex partners. For example, heterosexual female survivors may choose women as sexual partners because they can be more supportive of the healing process (e.g. offer more nurturance, security, and empathy). Homosexual female survivors may choose a male partner if their victimization experience interfered with an awareness of their sexual preference (Maltz and Holman, 1987).

The third significant aspect of sexuality that is disrupted by childhood sexual abuse is sexual functioning. Survivors often experience disorders of sexual arousal, response, and satisfaction. Many report that sexual arousal is associated with feelings experienced during the abuse (e.g. disgust, panic) or with trauma symptomatology (e.g. flashbacks).

Male survivors and sexuality

Although the sexual responses of males to victimization resemble the responses of female survivors in many ways, they are differentially influenced by male sex-role socialization and the frequency with which males are abused by males. Hyper-sexuality, compulsive sexual behaviours, and aggressive sexual behaviours may be exhibited by male survivors. Sexual identity concerns are frequently reported.

Counselling approaches to sexuality issues

Counselling related to sexuality can have an insight-oriented, cognitive, or behavioural focus. Initially, survivors need to make the connection between current sexual difficulties and their abuse experience, in much the same way as they do with other current difficulties. It is important to explore how their abuse experiences influenced their sexual development, their choice of sex partners, their sexual self-esteem, and their current sexual functioning.

Cognitive challenging or restructuring can be used to address the misconceptions of survivors regarding sex roles and sexuality (Becker et al., 1986; McCarthy, 1990; Westerlund, 1992). Maltz and Holman (1987) advised presenting the 'Bill of Sexual Rights' to survivors to challenge their sexual misconceptions. This 'Bill' includes basic premises, such as 'I have a right to my own body', 'I have a right to set my own sexual limits', and 'I have a right to experience sexual pleasure' (1987: 83). Westerlund (1992) recommended that counsellors encourage survivors to use self-affirming statements related to their body image and sexuality.

Maltz and Holman (1987) outlined several behavioural strategies that can help survivors deal with sexual problems. These include: avoidance of triggers of the abuse experience (e.g. the smell of alcohol, cigarette smoke) during sex, having sex in a place that is not similar to the place where the sexual abuse occurred, or learning to say no or to stop sexual activities with one's partner in a non-rejecting manner. Jehu (1990) recommended a coping skills training programme to address phobic responses to sexual stimuli. The programme includes relaxation training, guided self-dialogue, imagery rehearsal (systematic desensitization), and cognitive restructuring. Westerlund (1992) describes image stopping or alteration techniques to deal with intrusive material evoked during sexual activities.

Behaviourally oriented sex therapy to treat specific sexual dysfunctions is often indicated. Counsellors should generally acquire specific training to employ some of these procedures. Sex therapy techniques may include Masters and Johnson's (1970) squeeze technique for premature ejaculation (i.e., the head of the penis is squeezed by the partner to inhibit ejaculation), sensate focusing (i.e., the pairing of pleasurable sensations with relaxation) and graded sexual contact (i.e., engaging in sexual activities from the least to the most threatening) for orgasmic dysfunction and impotence, and desensitization (e.g. relaxation, hypnosis, self-vaginal dilation) for vaginismus.

Hunter (1995) discussed counselling issues with survivors who exhibit compulsive sexual behaviours, including voyeurism, exhibitionism, compulsive masturbation, bestiality, sadism, masochism, bondage/discipline, affairs, anonymous sex, telephone sex, frotteurism (indecent or invasive touch), the compulsive use of pornography, and cross-dressing. He argued that,

> Overall, the therapeutic task when treating those with sexual compulsiveness is to help clients determine what is the reasonable, acceptable goal of the behaviour and then to find new, less emotionally expensive methods to obtain the goal. For example, if one is lonely, it is certainly acceptable to seek the company of others. However, if the only relationship that has been available is that with a character in a pornographic film, the loneliness will continue and even increase once the film has ended. The client would benefit from having access to a therapy group or mutual-help group so that intimate, mutually rewarding relationships could be formed that will lead to a decrease in the client's loneliness. (1995: 78)

Bolton et al. (1989) outlined behavioural techniques used in the treatment of deviant sexual responses. Covert sensitization, for example, involves relaxation, hierarchy construction, and using imagery to pair deviant responses with aversive consequences.

If the survivor has a committed sexual partner, counselling related to issues of sexuality may include the partner at some point. Partners may experience feelings of rejection, powerlessness, intense anger toward the survivor's family, or inadequacy for not being able to make the survivor 'better'. The goals of couples treatment, therefore, may include: helping partners understand and appreciate the impact of the incest on the survivor's life; encouraging the couple to consider that the sexual dysfunction relates to the abuse, not to either partner's inadequacy; and assisting survivors in responding to their partners' needs and concerns (Maltz and Holman, 1987). Couples often need to learn to communicate openly with each other regarding their sexual issues. Sex therapy, using some of the techniques discussed above, often requires that both partners participate actively in treatment.

Case vignette

The following case vignette illustrates how counselling techniques may be combined to address a sexual dysfunction experienced by a female incest survivor. Grace was a 30-year-old woman who sought counselling for vaginismus. When she was a young child, Grace had been sexually abused by her father for several years. Because Grace originally did not connect her sexual dysfunction with her sexual abuse experience, this issue was addressed at the start of counselling.

> *Grace*: That [the abuse] happened so long ago. My problem now couldn't be related, could it?
>
> *Counsellor*: Often, one's sexual life can continue to be affected by an abuse experience. As a child who was sexually abused, you could not control or understand what was happening to you. Your body was violated and you were engaged in sexual activity you did not choose and were not ready for.
>
> *Grace*: Yes, maybe the tightening results from my not wanting to be violated again. But my boyfriend is kind, gentle.
>
> *Counsellor*: Yes, although as an adult you've chosen a caring partner, the act of sex can trigger old memories and feelings.
>
> *Grace*: Yes, sometimes after we try to have sex I do have nightmares. I have never truly enjoyed sex. Now that I have a nice boyfriend, I think I feel guilty. My father told me no one would love me for me. He called me a whore. Jack loves me, I know. But maybe I still feel dirty, after all these years.

Once Grace understood her sexual dysfunction in the larger context of her abuse experiences, more specific counselling interventions were used. Cognitive challenges were used to address Grace's belief that she was a 'whore' who did not deserve to have a good relationship or enjoyable sex. The belief that she had a right to sexual pleasure was extremely difficult for her to accept. She joined a women's sexuality group where this belief was reinforced by other group members. The use of relaxation techniques (e.g. warm baths, imagery) and self-vaginal dilation were used to treat the vaginismus. This symptom subsided after three months.

Survivors as offenders

For some survivors, the issue of sexual offending must be addressed. This issue may differ for female and male clients.

Lepine (1990) discussed her counselling experiences with female survivors who have also engaged in sexual offending behaviours. These women continued to experience overwhelming guilt even after working through survivor issues, and often would not disclose their offence to the counsellor for some time. Although the percentage of adult female survivors who subsequently sexually abuse others is believed to be very small, the author warned that counsellor denial of this possibility can interfere with the recovery of these survivors. Counsellors should neither minimize a survivor's guilt related to the offending behaviour nor 'join with, support, or exacerbate a disproportionate and disabling sense of guilt' (Lepine, 1990: 274). If the survivor was a child or adolescent at the time of the offence, the counsellor should help her consider the offence in the context of her developmental stage and her own abuse history.

Disclosure of offending behaviour is facilitated if clients have established a trusting relationship with the counsellor and if the counsellor introduces the issue. Lepine recommended an intervention such as: 'You know, when women have been sexually abused as children, they sometimes act out sexually against others, too' (1990: 275). The counsellor should respond calmly to a survivor's disclosure of offending behaviour. He or she should non-judgmentally convey the message that, while the behaviour is unacceptable, the counsellor will not reject the client and will assist her in dealing with this issue. In certain instances (e.g. the ongoing abuse of a child), this might mean reporting the offence.

Counselling must address the survivor's feelings of guilt about abusing another person. Lepine (1990) recommended the use of the empty-chair technique, in which survivors speak vicariously with their victims. Survivors may acknowledge the offence and its consequences, apologize and ask for forgiveness, and share their own abuse experience. They may also communicate these messages to their victims through the use of the unsent letter. Actual contact with a victim, however, should be thoughtfully considered before being carried out. Issues to be explored include: the survivor's motives (e.g. survivors should not expect the victim to resolve their guilt); the consequences (e.g. legal actions, the survivor's reputation); the victim's potential reactions (e.g. trauma symptomatology if the experience had been repressed); and the survivor's potential reactions.

The counselling of male survivors who have engaged in sexually offending behaviour has also been addressed. In many cases, the typical disclosure process differs from that of female survivors. Female survivors often begin counselling to deal with their abuse, and later in the process reveal the offending behaviour. Male survivors, on the other hand, often enter counselling because of a sexual offence, and reveal their own victimization experience later in the process. These differences may reflect social role expectations. Because women are socialized to care for and protect others, offending behaviours may be less frequent, less traumatic, and more likely to cease when they are adults (Lepine, 1990). Males, who are socialized to act out their feelings and deny their experience of victimization, may be more likely to offend into adulthood in ways that will result in some contact with the criminal justice system.

The percentage of male victims who become offenders is unclear. However, the assumption that most male survivors engage in sexually offending behaviours is a destructive myth that can interfere with the healing of survivors. Gerber suggested that, 'It seems more reasonable to acknowledge that according to research, it [transition from victim to offender] occurs with some frequency and causation is attributable to a variety of variables' (1990:. 154). Childhood sexual abuse factors associated with later offending behaviours include: bizarre sexual acts, sexual acts accompanied by the threat of violence, the use of a 'seductive, covert, pre-sexual conditioning process' (1990: 155) by the offender, and a long duration of abuse. Certain personality characteristics (e.g. passive dependency) and chemical dependency are also thought to contribute to the transition from victim to offender.

The counselling of male survivors who are also perpetrators requires that both the offending behaviour and the childhood sexual abuse be addressed. Counselling typically begins with perpetrator issues and progresses to issues related to childhood victimization. Counselling offenders may occur in four stages, which are described by Carlson (1990).

The first stage is the focus on perpetrator characteristics, attitudes, and self-concept. Counselling interventions include: setting limits; providing structure; and confronting the perpetrator's denial, his view of himself as a victim of the system or of his family, and his tendency to project negative characteristics on to others (e.g. calling his abused daughter a 'slut').

The next stage in counselling is the reinforcement of the client's positive characteristics and the development of his strengths. Counselling interventions include assisting the survivor to develop extra-familial support systems, strengthen his own boundaries (e.g. develop assertiveness skills), and learn to delay gratification. Counsellors should reinforce other positive behaviours, such as the survivor's accepting responsibility for his actions, expressing his feelings, and communicating his needs in a direct manner.

The next stage, treating the 'victim within', occurs when issues related to the client's victimization begin to emerge. During this stage, the counsellor provides support, education, and validation related to the client's victimization experiences. The client is encouraged to describe these experiences fully. He can then appreciate that his own victimization was a source of his victimizing behaviour, although this does not relieve him of the responsibility for his offences. When the survivor gets in touch with his own feelings of victimization, he can begin to develop empathy for his victims.

The final stage of counselling is called 'returning the parental role', as the client again assumes responsibility for his own behaviour. He begins to set his own boundaries (e.g. respecting others' privacy, determining appropriate limits with his children) and to determine for himself what constitute appropriate sexual behaviours. He also identifies available sources of support following treatment, methods by which he will care for himself, and a plan of action if he feels he is in danger of reoffending.

Case example

The case of Jerry, who was discussed in the preceding chapter, exemplifies the process of making desired life changes once the connections between childhood experiences and adult functioning have been made. Jerry made changes in his self-concept, his relationships with his wife and family of origin, and his job.

Much of counselling focused on Jerry's self-esteem. Jerry originally described himself as an 'insignificant failure'. He also believed himself to be 'unmanly', a self-perception that was probably related to his abuse experiences involving same-sex offenders. The following client–counsellor interaction, based on Peplau's model (O'Toole and Welt, 1989), shows how self-esteem issues were addressed with Jerry:

> *Jerry*: I guess I'm not much of anything. I'm certainly not much of a man. [Self-view in awareness]
> *Counsellor*: Where did you get the message that you are not much of anything?
> *Jerry*: I guess from my family. My dad never bothered with me much, except to yell when he was drunk, or to tell me what to do at work. My mom, well, she thought it best we kids be 'seen and not heard'. She was pretty weak. I wanted more to do with her but she was always sick.
> *Counsellor*: So both of your parents gave you the message, in one way or another, that you were not very important. Tell me about an experience you had when you felt particularly unimportant.
> *Jerry*: Once, I brought home a table I made in shop, you know, wood-working class. I thought it was good. I put it in the living room. I thought my mom would be happy but instead she had me put it out in the garage so my dad 'wouldn't be upset with such clutter'. I was disappointed because the instructor had said the table was really good.

Counsellor: I can see why a young boy would not feel very important in this situation. Something you made yourself, which had received praise, was discarded in the interest of keeping your dad calm.

Jerry: Yes, and shop was the only thing I was really good in. [Maybe me self-view]

Counsellor: You had a talent that was not recognized by your parents, but was recognized by your teacher. Were there other situations like this – instances when your parents did not attend to you, but others did?

Jerry: Jean, of course. She was good to me, until she left home. No one else until Jane . . .

Counsellor: Although your parents gave you the message you weren't very important, Jean, and later Jane, showed that you were important to them.

Jerry described receiving messages from his parents indicating that he was not considered a significant member of the family, and that it was best if he just stayed out of the way. Once Jerry recognized that his self-perceptions stemmed from these messages rather than from his own inherent worthlessness, he considered other ways of viewing himself. He concluded that he was special to Jean, who clearly cared for him a great deal. He was thus worthwhile in someone's eyes. Jerry also gradually began to consider his strengths – that he had survived his childhood, had maintained a basically sound marriage, and had developed many skills related to his trade. Some of these views were associated with anxiety as they were incongruent with Jerry's accustomed self-perceptions. For example, Jerry was initially very resistant to considering himself a skillful tradesperson as this meant he might be valued outside the family shop and, therefore, vocational opportunities might exist for him away from his family.

Eventually, Jerry was seen in counselling with his wife Jane. He had never told her of the abuse, and chose to do so during a counselling session. She was extremely supportive, although some tension did develop between Jane and Jerry when she expressed anger toward his family, whom she 'never liked anyway'. She had trouble understanding why Jerry should have any loyalty remaining toward them. Nonetheless, she was able to assure Jerry that she did not blame him for the infertility, nor did she see him as 'unmanly'. She did, however, need him to understand her feelings of loss. Once Jerry stopped blaming himself for the infertility, he was able to be more emotionally available to her. Jerry felt unable, however, to 'talk about his feelings', as this was discouraged in his family of origin. Thus, the development of new communication skills became the focus of couple counselling. Both Jerry and Jane became more successful in expressing their needs and feelings in ways the other could hear. Because their sexual relationship improved as their communication skills developed, the couple did not require behaviourally-oriented sex therapy.

Jerry chose not to confront his parents or his brother Tom about the abuse, but did identify the need to separate from his family. He made the difficult decision to leave the machine shop, and began work at a different plant. He interacted with his family only occasionally, when he chose to do so. He did well in his new position and was ultimately appointed as shift supervisor.

8

Addressing Resolution Issues

O nce survivors have begun to successfully employ new coping mechanisms and make desired life changes, they often deal with issues related to the resolution of the childhood sexual abuse experience. Resolution does not indicate that the experience of abuse is forgotten, or that the healing process is finished. Indeed, many survivors believe that healing can be a lifelong process (Draucker, 1992b). Resolution refers to the process by which the childhood sexual abuse experience is integrated into the individual's identity, but is no longer the primary force that guides his or her adult life. Sgroi (1989a) refers to this as relinquishing the survivor identity. The individual views himself or herself from a variety of perspectives. The issues discussed below are frequently related to the process of resolution.

Forgiveness

After clients have experienced some healing from the sexual abuse experience, many struggle with the issue of whether or not to forgive the offender. Some survivors believe that forgiveness is a prerequisite to true recovery; others believe they must forgive the offender because of their religious or social beliefs. It can be important for counsellors to help clients determine what forgiveness means to them. Maltz and Holman (1987) discussed two styles of forgiveness. In the first style, survivors release the offender from responsibility for the abuse because they have determined that the offender's actions were justifiable in some way. Such forgiveness may represent a survivor's attempts to deny repressed anger, hurt, or betrayal toward the offender, and may be a form of self-blame or minimization. The second style of forgiveness involves coming to appreciate the offender's 'humanness, limitations, and history' (1987: 31). This may include achieving an understanding of the offender's own childhood abuse experiences or his or her adult weaknesses or pathology. The authors suggest that this style of forgiveness can be beneficial for survivors, as it can help them develop compassion and forgiveness for themselves.

Hall and Lloyd (1989) suggested that forgiveness occurs when survivors accept their feelings related to the abuse, especially their anger, but no longer seek revenge. This type of forgiveness can free survivors from their ties to the offender. If they no longer need to avenge the offence, the offender becomes less relevant in their healing process; survivors can then begin to accept responsibility for their adult happiness.

The survivors' religious or philosophical beliefs related to forgiveness must be discussed, acknowledged, and respected. Forgiveness, however, that stems from true acceptance of one's feelings, insight into the offender's childhood experiences and adult limitations, and personal healing that has moved one beyond the need for revenge is usually more therapeutic than forgiveness that is dictated by religious or social prescriptions.

Counsellors can help clients determine the personal meaning they attach to forgiveness and the role forgiveness might play in their healing. They may choose, for example, to forgive a non-offending parent, but not the offender. Counsellors should stress that forgiveness is not a prerequisite to their healing, but a personal choice some survivors may make as they begin to move toward a resolution of their abuse experience.

The following client–counsellor interaction illustrates a survivor's struggle with the issue of forgiveness. Pamela is a 23-year-old woman who was sexually abused as a child by her older brother.

Pamela: My visit [to her family] did not go well this weekend. I was talking to my mother and she said she believes to be truly healed I must forgive my brother. She's brought this up before.
Counsellor: What is it like for you when your mom says this?
Pamela: I get really angry. I think she wants this whole thing to be over and done with so he can come back into our lives, and we can pretend it [the abuse] never happened. I don't know, though, maybe at some point I will be able to forgive him. Not now, but at some point maybe. I don't know.
Counsellor: You were angry at your mom because you sense her push for you to forgive your brother comes more from her needs to reunite the family than from her concern about your healing?
Pamela: Yes, all along she has been more concerned about getting things back to normal. I'm not saying I'll never forgive him. I'm just not ready yet. And I don't want to be pushed. But some day I hope I will reach a point of forgiveness.
Counsellor: People mean different things when they talk about forgiveness. When you say at some point you may be able to forgive your brother, what do you mean?

Pamela: Well, not that I'll say that the abuse was OK. I'll never say that. It wasn't. It hurt me deeply and that will never change. Maybe at some point, though, I won't feel as much hatred. At one point, I wanted him dead. I know he did to me what was done to him. Yet, that doesn't make it OK. I don't know. I'm confused.

Counsellor: Yes, one meaning of forgiveness is that one forgives and forgets the abuse, coming to believe it was unimportant and should be forgotten. Perhaps you believe this is what your mom wants you to do. Another meaning of forgiveness is that one reaches some understanding of why the abuse occurred, and then moves beyond needing retribution. One can still feel angry, but no longer be driven by bitterness.

Pamela: Yes, it was somehow helpful to know Grandpa abused Tim [her brother]. Although that didn't make what he did to me OK, it somehow helped make things make sense, if you know what I mean. I would like to be able to be in the same room with him without freaking. Maybe then I'll feel more like he can't pull my strings any longer.

Reintegrating into the family of origin

Many survivors discontinue or limit contact with their family of origin when they begin the healing process. In some cases, survivors need distance from the dysfunctional nature of their family in order to appreciate how the family dynamics influenced their development. Some survivors break off contact because family members continue to engage in behaviours that are deleterious to the their recovery (e.g. blaming the survivor for the abuse, disapproving of the survivor's therapy). For example, one survivor in the incest healing study (Draucker, 1992b) reported that, 'I didn't talk to my family for two years. I withdrew from them after a really severe confrontation about counselling, which they really objected to.'

After they have experienced some healing, many survivors decide to re-establish contact with their family of origin. The same survivor stated:

And as soon as my counselling sessions had ended, I found out my mom had cancer, so it was like, you were able to spend two years away in healing and getting over it, then it was like time to go back and slay the dragons and see my brothers and sisters and talk to my mom and try and work through some of the problems and feelings that I had with them, which I thought I did pretty well.

Survivors need to approach their family from the perspective of the changes they have made in the healing process, rather than interacting with their family based on old roles and patterns. Participants in the incest healing study stressed that the re-establishment of contact with their family had to be, in some way, on the survivors' terms, which were often specific and definite. One woman maintained a relationship with her brother, the offender, as long as he remained in therapy. Another participant, who had been abused by her stepfather, discussed re-establishing a relationship with her mother, which she planned to discontinue if her mother engaged in any of the hurtful or destructive behaviours from which she had agreed to refrain (e.g. blaming the survivor for the abuse).

Reintegrating into the family of origin, based on changes the client has made, can be an important resolution issue. It is helpful to explore whether a client has any unrealistic expectations related to his or her family, such as that the family will have changed to meet the client's needs. Typically, families will attempt to repeat old, familiar patterns to maintain the status quo. Survivors should guard against allowing the actions of their families once again to control their sense of well-being. Counselling may be helpful in assisting survivors to maintain realistic expectations regarding their family's responses, while focusing on what survivors can control when re-entering the family or re-establishing a relationship with a family member.

Davis (1990) proposed an activity that assists survivors in establishing new ground rules or setting limits when interacting with their families. She asks survivors to determine what things they would no longer do with their family (e.g. care for an inebriated parent), as well as what things they will no longer discuss with their family (e.g. the survivor's sexual life). Davis also encourages survivors to specify the conditions under which they will have contact with their family (e.g. only at the survivor's residence; at the family's home, only if the offender is not present). Counsellors can also discuss how clients can best communicate these ground rules to their family, what the experience of setting limits might be like for them, what their contingency plan will be if the ground rules are not respected, and how they anticipate their family will respond. Family members will usually test the limits; survivors should be prepared for this.

It is most important that survivors do not engage in old family dynamics in which they are exploited, manipulated, ignored, or belittled. In some instances, contact continues to be destructive and survivors may again choose to break off their relationship with the family. This decision is often accompanied by sadness and grief, feelings that must be validated by the counsellor. Letting go of the family of origin or coming to terms with its limitations can be a significant part of the resolution process.

Finding meaning in the experience

Taylor (1983) theorized that one way to cope with a traumatic or a victimizing event is to search for meaning in the experience. She defined the search for meaning as 'an effort to understand the event: why it happened and what impact it has had' (1983: 1161). Research has suggested that this is important for sexual abuse survivors and may facilitate the resolution of the abuse experience (Draucker, 1989, 1995, 1997; Silver et al., 1983).

Understanding the cause of the event is referred to as causal attribution. This process has been discussed primarily in relation to survivors' reattributing the cause of the abuse from themselves to the offender. Although holding the offender responsible for the abuse is important in addressing issues of self-blame, it does not seem to be sufficient explanation for many survivors. Many question why the offender did what he or she did, why the abuse occurred in their family, and, ultimately, why society permits the widespread occurrence of childhood sexual abuse.

In the study of incest survivors (Draucker, 1992b), many participants indicated that they had answered these questions for themselves. Several reported that they had learned that their offenders were impaired in some way (e.g. alcoholic, psychotic). One participant said, 'My father was an alcoholic who was raised in a time when women were inferior. He was also sick.' Other clients attributed the actions of the offenders to the offenders' own history of abuse. One stated: '[It was my] older brother taking out aggressions on me, most likely caused by his own molestation from our paternal grandmother.' Several survivors attributed the cause of the abuse to family dynamics. For example, a participant stated, 'I realize that the incest experience was because of my dysfunctional family, not because of me.' One survivor placed the blame for the incest on society, saying that she had come to believe that the incest was part of 'an extreme exploitation of females commonly practiced in the USA'.

Whether or not certain types of attribution are more helpful in facilitating healing is uncertain. What is important in regard to resolution of trauma is that individuals come up with a causal explanation that is satisfactory to them. Janoff-Bulman (1992: 127) argued that attributions fit 'into the larger, richer efforts of survivors to rebuild their inner world following traumatic life events. This is only one piece of the greater picture, yet it is a reflection of the larger task – to integrate their victimization by somehow getting it to fit better with prior self- and world-views.'

In the late phase of counselling, survivors often seek closure on the question of why they were abused. In some cases, it is helpful for the counsellor to provide factual or theoretical material to aid in this quest. For example, discussing incestuous family dynamics, as outlined by Gelinas (1983), may help survivors understand the functioning of their family. Discussing incest from a feminist perspective (e.g. according to Herman, 1981) may help survivors put their childhood sexual abuse in a larger societal context. Reading literature can also facilitate this. Daugherty (1984), for example, wrote a book for survivors of childhood sexual abuse entitled *Why me?* In one chapter, the author addresses the issue of understanding individuals who sexually abuse children. This helps survivors with their need to know why the abuser did what he or she did.

Taylor (1983) also indicated that in order to find meaning, one must understand the significance the traumatic event has had in one's life. She suggested that this could involve construing positive meaning from the experience by reappraising one's life, developing a new attitude toward life, or gaining increased self-knowledge. Survivors of childhood sexual abuse who participated in a survey study on coping (Draucker, 1992a) described these processes as part of healing. They indicated that, because of the abuse, they are stronger, more self-reliant, or independent; have a greater self-awareness of their emotional or spiritual life; have acquired a sense of purpose in life; or have developed a better understanding of human nature in general. Wiehe, who conducted a survey of 150 victims of sibling abuse, reported that some of the respondents saw a 'silver lining in the dark cloud of their abuse' (1990: 132) and used their abuse experience for personal growth.

Resolving the abuse issue may involve the 'rethinking of one's attitude or priorities to restructure one's life along more satisfying lines' (Taylor, 1983: 1163). This does not mean that survivors conclude that they were glad the abuse occurred, or that the offender actually 'did them a favour' and is, therefore, exonerated. Rather, they conclude that the abuse was a negative experience, but from that experience, or from the healing after that experience, they were able to grow personally in some way. One survivor (Draucker, 1992b) stated, 'It [the abuse] has forced my growth in areas that would have been neglected otherwise. I have to examine how much of our behaviour is choice versus reactions – where's the balance?'

In the following client–counsellor interaction, a survivor struggles with the issue of finding meaning in her incest experience. Rosalie is a 55-year-old woman who was sadistically sexually abused as a child by her uncle.

Rosalie: You know, I realized that as much suffering as I have experienced – it's been almost 50 years of suffering – I don't think I would be as strong as I am today if it hadn't been for what he did.
Counsellor: In what ways are you stronger than you would have been?
Rosalie: After being in therapy, I now know that I can handle just about anything. If I lived through what I did as a youngster, I can live through anything. I never realized that before. My friend Eleanor falls apart at every family crisis. In fact, the other day someone called me a 'tough cookie'. I think that's true. I am a tough cookie. I wouldn't wish what happened to me on a dog, but it did make me strong.
Counsellor: So having survived a horrible experience as a child . . .
Rosalie: Yes, I survived because I was strong. I feel good about myself now. I like who I am. Someone asked me if I'm glad the abuse happened. That's nonsense. Of course I'm not glad. I work to stop abuse. But it was one of the many things that made me who I am today. And I like me.

Narrative therapy

Narrative therapy, based on the work of Michael White and David Epston (White, 1989, 1992, 1995; White and Epston, 1990), is a counselling approach that addresses the issue of finding meaning in misfortune. Several authors (Adams-Wescott and Isenbart, 1996; Draucker, 1998) suggest that this approach may be particularly applicable to individuals who have experienced significant interpersonal victimization throughout their lives. According to Adams-Wescott and Isenbart, 'The narrative therapist is interested in the meaning the young person ascribes to the experience of abuse and how this meaning influences the story he or she develops about self' (1996: 14).

The narrative approach is based on the concept of social construction, that each individual's reality is constructed through interaction with others and institutions. Interpersonal conversations are internalized and organized into stories through which we interpret our experiences (White and Epston, 1990). Individuals may internalize the dominant cultural narratives that shape and maintain the distribution of power in society (Freedman and Combs, 1996). Dominant narratives, often reflecting oppressive sociopolitical forces, lead individuals to participate in stories that are dissatisfying, constraining, and disempowering. Narrative therapy seeks to create a space for new stories.

White discussed how to free clients from the constraints of a destructive narrative by locating the problem outside the person, a process called externalization. White explained, 'Externalization is an approach to therapy that encourages persons to objectify, and at times, to personify the problem they experience as oppressive' (1989: 5). Individuals in counselling are encouraged to explore unique outcomes – i.e, moments when their lives were not disrupted by their problem, when the problem did not occur, or when the problem was overcome. Hidden strengths and competencies are revealed; individuals are free to rewrite their stories.

Adams-Wescott and Isenbart indicated that unique outcomes for clients who were molested as children 'include events from the person's lived experience that contradict stories of personal deficits and permanent damage' (1996: 16). Rather than focusing on pathology, clients are invited to discuss events that represent their struggle against the effects of abuse. Once free to experiment with preferred narratives, they may escape victim life stories and construct stories of personal agency. Draucker suggested this approach 'challenges sociopolitical conditions that contribute to violence, highlights women's personal insurrections against these conditions, and supports the reauthoring of life stories' (1998: 168).

The process of helping others

The need to help others who have been abused, or the need to make the world a safer place more generally, seems to be a key part of the resolution process for many survivors. In the incest healing study (Draucker, 1992b), for example, the majority of participants identified that having a positive impact on their world – by helping other victims personally, being an advocate for victims, or choosing a helping vocation (e.g. teaching) – was an important aspect of their own recovery. In a study that investigated the process of construing benefit from a negative experience of incest, Draucker (1992a) found that the majority of survivors who derived any benefit from the experience listed the ability to help others as a positive outcome. As a result of their incest experience, these women indicated that they were able to help others in ways that non-abused individuals could not. They had acquired a special ability to empathize with those who were suffering, the courage to speak out against injustice, a unique skill to detect abuse in their work settings (e.g. a paediatric emergency room), and a particular vigilance, which they used to protect their own children from abuse.

Helping activities seem to be beneficial for survivors only when they have worked through a number of issues in their own healing process (e.g. caretaking issues, setting boundaries with others, dealing with issues of blame). For example, it can be a devastating experience for survivors to speak publicly about their abuse when they have not worked through their feelings of shame. If survivors choose to help other survivors before they have learned to define their own boundaries or to set interpersonal limits, they tend to feel burdened or overwhelmed. The counsellor may help survivors explore the role that helping others can play in the healing process, and support these activities when they contribute to the resolution of the abuse experience.

Addressing identity issues

The key resolution issue for incest survivors is establishing a clear sense of their own identities. Much of the healing process has focused on giving up the role of victim by taking control of one's own thoughts, feelings, and actions. When survivors perceive that they have given up this role, they often mourn the loss; the victim role probably defined their identities for some time. Along with the role of the victim, survivors also often abandon caretaking roles they find oppressive. These roles may have shaped their interpersonal relationships and perhaps even their vocational choices. Counselling may provide survivors with an opportunity to deal with feelings of loss and anxiety associated with these changes.

Sgroi (1989a) maintained that, ultimately, clients can also give up the survivor identity. They recognize their strengths and weaknesses, and integrate the sexual abuse experience into their total identities. They have found success in adopting new coping mechanisms and have assumed responsibility for their own happiness; therefore, they no longer need to define themselves by their childhood sexual abuse experience. Sgroi (1989a) suggested that this stage can be elusive for survivors. In the later stages of treatment, counsellors might discuss the process of giving up the survivor identity. One participant in the incest healing study (Draucker, 1992b) discussed this:

Another thing I think I dealt with was to try to get rid of the role of incest survivor. I used to play with it by saying, no, I was a survivor. Because of it, a lot of good things were given to me. I understand, I could empathize, I could do a lot of things that way and I was a survivor. I was getting on with my life and all that. . . . Dr Susan Forward was in this area and a lot of women were calling [to a radio programme] and she would talk to them and she had been an incest victim herself and had written a book which I had read and her idea was to get out of the role of being an incest survivor and do your life without having to be in that role. I liked that idea. I worked very hard on trying to just not constantly come from, dwell on, be, an incest survivor.

Termination of counselling

Along with resolution comes the process of terminating of counselling. This, of course, can represent a significant loss for the survivor, but also a transition consistent with relinquishing the survivor identity. The termination process may include: a review of the healing process, reminiscence about the highlights of counselling, sharing of feelings between counsellor and client regarding the relationship and termination, and an exploration of the client's future plans. Many counsellors choose to extend an invitation to survivors to keep in touch with them because survivors often profit from sharing ongoing life changes with the counsellor.

Case example

The following case exemplifies how reintegrating into the family of origin can be related to resolution for survivors.

Candy was a 22-year-old college student who had attended counselling for approximately one year to deal with having been sexually abused by her brother, Ken. The abuse occurred intermittently for approximately a year, when she was 7 and he was 15. The sexual activities primarily included genital fondling, although Candy believed vaginal penetration was attempted on some occasions. Ken had been adopted at the age of two, at a time when Candy's parents believed they could not have any biological children. Ken exhibited significant behavioural problems (e.g. being expelled from school, minor scrapes with the law, unruliness at home) throughout most of his childhood. He was ultimately diagnosed as having foetal alcohol syndrome. As an adult, he continued to live with his parents, worked at a local service station, and spent most of his time with his local 'buddies'.

After being in counselling for over six months, Candy decided to tell her parents about the abuse during one of her visits home. She reported to her counsellor that her father responded only by saying, 'I should kill him next time I see him.' Candy's mother initially became 'hysterical' and was unable to discuss Candy's experience with her. However, on their next contact, Candy's mother began to defend Ken and minimize the abuse. She suggested to Candy that the abuse was normal child's play, that Ken probably did not mean any harm, and that perhaps the counsellor was making too big a deal of the issue. Candy's father would not discuss the abuse further.

Although Candy had spent time in counselling preparing for this disclosure, she stated that she was nonetheless devastated by her parents' response and decided to limit her weekly visits with them. Initially, she would see them occasionally, on major holidays; when holiday visits became stressful, she ceased these visits as well. Candy's mother wrote to her frequently, begging her to come home. Her mother's letters often contained references to her ill-health and despondency over Candy's break from the family.

Her parents' reactions to her disclosure prompted Candy to examine their roles as non-offending parents. Although she had initially assumed that they had no knowledge of the abuse, she eventually began to wonder if her mother 'knew on some level'. Candy believed that she did not tell her mother about the abuse at the time it occurred because her mother pampered Ken. As a child, Candy believed her mother would fall apart if she knew 'what her children were doing'. Candy stated that she would never have considered telling her father, who was seldom at home and who would not 'talk about personal things anyway'.

Candy struggled for some time in counselling to understand her parents' role in the abuse situation, as well as their reactions to her disclosure of the abuse. This led to a discussion of her parents' family backgrounds. Candy reported that her mother grew up in poverty and was raised by several aunts, at least two of whom worked as prostitutes. She had spent her later years in a foster home and met her husband, Candy's father, during her last year of high school. Candy knew less of her father's history, other than that he came from a strict, but 'respectable', military family. Candy's parents tried to have a child for many years and finally adopted Ken through a Catholic adoption agency. Candy herself was a 'late miracle' baby.

Candy indicated that her mother always seemed overwhelmed by child-care responsibilities with Ken: 'She was always going to school or to court or to counselling to deal with his problems.' Candy suspected that her mother had become overly involved with her son, whereas her father withdrew, having little to do with Ken or with the family. Candy, as a child, was quiet and caused no problems. As an adolescent, she became her mother's confidante. Her mother frequently complained to Candy about the lack of support she received from Candy's dad, a 'workaholic', and the troubles she continued to have with Ken.

Candy surmised that her mother had probably married her father to gain the respectability and stability she lacked as a child.

Although her mother's marriage provided those things, her father showed little nurturance and caring. When Ken began to have problems, her mother took total responsibility for him. Candy guessed that her mother probably felt like a failure because she had invested so much in having the 'all-American' family and was unable to 'make Ken better'. As Ken's problems increased, her father withdrew further, adding to her mother's feelings of burden and abandonment. Her pregnancy with Candy, which at one time would have been welcomed, was unplanned and probably added to her mother's stress.

After achieving some understanding of these dynamics, Candy decided to resume contact with her mother. In the following interaction, she and the counsellor discuss this issue:

> *Candy*: I have decided to see my mom again. I feel better myself and I miss her. I don't need to see Dad, but I do want to see Mom. I've been away long enough. When I see her though, I'm afraid I'll slip back. That's what kept me from calling her. I've come so far myself. But I also want to talk with her about some of what we've been talking about, you know, her background and stuff.
>
> *Counsellor*: I know you've been wanting to be involved with your mom again; it's important to you. In what ways are you afraid you'll slip back if you see her again?
>
> *Candy*: Well, it hurt me so much last time when my mom defended Ken and made light of the abuse. Then she got sick. Remember . . . I got real depressed. That could happen again. That's why I hope she's changed.
>
> *Counsellor*: We discussed your mom's response when you told her about the sexual abuse and I know you've determined that her defence of Ken and denial of the abuse probably results from her long-standing need to have a normal, perfect family and that it is her pattern to withdraw from her problems by becoming ill.
>
> *Candy*: I know, but maybe she's changed and can face it now. Maybe my staying away shook her up enough . . . Maybe she'll stand up to my brother to show me she really believes he did something wrong. That would help me and she says she wants to help me.
>
> *Counsellor*: Facing the abuse and dealing with your brother in a way that would be helpful for you would be a major change in your mom's way of dealing with things . . .
>
> *Candy*: Yes, it's highly unlikely, I know.
>
> *Counsellor*: You are hoping for a significant change. Although your mom loves you and may sincerely want to help you, there is a strong pull for family members to stay the same. To change is threatening.
>
> *Candy*: I so wish she would be different. She probably won't be. I guess I know that on some level.
>
> *Counsellor*: When you resume contact with your family, you cannot make them change in ways you would like them to. No one has that control over others. You may hope for certain changes while also considering what's realistic.

Candy: I'm afraid if I go back, and she hasn't changed, she'll just make light of the whole thing again.

Counsellor: Although you cannot control how your mom responds to you, you can control how you respond to her.

Candy: I know what's coming. [*Smiles*] Because she makes light of the whole thing, I don't have to.

Counsellor: Yes, you've made many changes. One change is that you no longer blame yourself for what happened. You seem to hold that belief very strongly now. You accept that the abuse was a traumatic event in your life. Your mom cannot take that away.

Candy: No, she cannot. I do believe that. I guess I also know that without some kind of help, like counselling, she won't change. That makes me sad. I wish she would get help, to understand what did happen to me, and to help herself as well. Otherwise, although I'll never blame myself again, if she defends Ken, I will get frustrated with her and probably stay away again. If only she would get help, I think that's the only way we can be really close again.

Counsellor: Although you cannot make her go to counselling, you can ask her to do that and decide how you will proceed with your relationship based on her response.

Candy: Yes, she needs counselling before we really get back together.

This interaction reaffirmed Candy's belief that the abuse was a significant, traumatic experience, and that contact with her mother could no longer jeopardize this belief. She concluded, however, that her mother would need to confront what had happened to Candy before they could have a meaningful relationship. Candy agreed to have contact with her mother at this point only if her mother agreed to attend counselling. Although her mother consented to this and found a counsellor she liked, she was extremely reluctant and missed several early sessions due to illness. She eventually became very involved with counselling, however. With the support of her counsellor, she confirmed much of what Candy had inferred about her mother's background. Her mother shared with Candy that she had suspected the abuse but could not face it. She confessed that she had feared that if her husband had found out what Ken was doing, he would have forced Ken to leave the home, something he often threatened to do as Ken's problems increased. At this point, Candy expressed anger toward her mother because she had chosen to protect Ken rather than Candy. Her mother was not only able to tolerate Candy's expression of anger, but admitted that she had, in fact, sacrificed Candy due to her own limitations and fears (e.g. of her husband, of Ken, of what others would think). This event was significant for Candy as it cemented many of the issues she had addressed earlier in counselling related to her own self-blame. Her mother also acknowledged that she believed that the abuse was a traumatic experience for Candy and she deeply regretted not intervening to stop it.

Candy eventually agreed to visit the family home again, something she had not done since her initial disclosure of the abuse to her parents. In the following client–counsellor interaction, Candy discusses her concerns about visiting her family in their home, and decides what ground rules she wishes to establish.

Candy: My parents want me to come home and I want to go there, I think, I'm not sure. My brother will be there and I'm not ready to see him yet. He's loud and butts into all our conversations, whether they involve him or not. He invades my space. Everyone just puts up with it. Also, I'm ready to see my dad, I think, but I feel really uncomfortable because my mother fusses over him so. She waits on him hand and foot. I'll be expected to do that too. You know, bring him coffee, soda, when he can get it himself. My mother does this for my brother sometimes as well. It makes me sick.

Counsellor: You are concerned, then, that if you go home things will be the way they were before. And that you will fall into old habits, such as putting up with your brother's behaviour or waiting on your father.

Candy: Yes, but now I couldn't stand doing those things.

Counsellor: Yes, because you've made changes. Putting up with your brother's behaviour is a passive thing to do, and you've been working on actively setting limits on the intrusive behaviours of others. Waiting on your dad is a deferent behaviour, also something you've been working on avoiding.

Candy: I'm so afraid in that house I'll fall back into doing those things.

Counsellor: Again, you cannot control what others do, but you can decide what you will or will not do and what you will or will not tolerate there.

Candy: OK, then, I decide here and now that I will not wait on my dad or my brother. And I will tell them this up-front.

Counsellor: Yes, you cannot decide if your mother will wait on them, but you can decide whether you will or not. What will it be like for you to set this limit?

Candy: It was scary when I heard myself saying it. But it feels good. I know I can do it. I can say no. 'Dad, I will not get your coffee when I'm visiting.' Wow. That felt good. If they don't accept that, I'll leave. My brother is a different story, though. I think his very presence will bother me a lot. Especially since I'm not ready to confront him about the abuse.

Counsellor: What would you like to do about your brother?

Candy: Really, I don't want to see him at all.

Counsellor: How can you have that happen?

Candy: Well, I can visit when he's not there. I can agree to go only when he's out. A ground rule will be that if Ken's there, I won't be. I won't have him there until I'm ready. If Mom wants me home, she'll have to ensure that Ken will not be there.

Candy identified unhealthy family patterns in which she no longer wanted to participate and determined how to avoid such participation by specifying what she would not do (i.e., wait on the men in the family) and by establishing an important ground rule (i.e., she would not visit when her brother was present). On several occasions, Candy recognized attempts by family members to test her limits. For example, during one visit her mother was carrying a coffee cup to her dad in the living room and stopped to answer the phone. Without saying a word, she handed the cup to Candy. At that point, Candy realized she could put the cup down or bring it to her father. She chose to put the cup on the counter, reinforcing her choice not to wait on him. On one occasion, the family 'forgot' to make arrangements for Ken to be away from the home for Candy's visit. Consistent with her contingency plan, Candy left immediately and visited a high school friend instead of spending the afternoon with her family.

Eventually, Candy chose to confront Ken about the abuse. He responded by becoming sullen and withdrawn, but did not deny the abuse had occurred. Candy grew very aware of his limitations and, although she did not address the issue of forgiveness, she claimed that she had got in touch with how 'pathetic' her brother had become.

After this confrontation, Candy began to visit her family less frequently, having decided that she needed to work on developing friendships at school. She was now withdrawing from her family because it was the 'normal thing to do at [my] age'. However, she believed that reintegrating into her family in a healthy way (e.g. by no longer keeping the incest secret, by setting limits based on her own needs) gave her the freedom to move on and establish her own adult relationships.

9

Group Counselling

G roup counselling for survivors of childhood sexual abuse is
an effective treatment modality, especially when used in
conjunction with individual counselling. Receiving support and
confrontation from those who have shared similar life experiences
and having the opportunity to help others can be especially
powerful for survivors. This chapter will address the goals of
group counselling, types of survivor group, factors to consider in
planning a group, and issues that often arise as groups progress.

Goals of group counselling

Although different types of survivor group may have various
specific goals, many groups have several goals in common. These
include: decreasing feelings of isolation, stigma, and shame; challenging survivors' perceptions of themselves as different; increasing feelings of self-esteem; instilling hope for recovery; developing
trust in others; practising interpersonal skills; and developing a
social support network. As mentioned in Chapter 2, survivor
groups are not recommended for clients with no clear memories of
abuse. Due to social compliance and suggestion, group involvement may increase the risk of false memory production (Courtois,
1999).

Types of survivor group

There are basically two types of group for individuals who were
sexually abused as children. Survivors may participate in a self-
help support group or in a professionally led clinical group. There
are several different formats used in clinical groups. When planning to run a survivor group or when referring clients to a group,
counsellors should consider the pros and cons of the type and
format of the group to determine whether it will meet the needs of
their clients.

Support groups

Self-help support groups are organized by survivors themselves and operate without a clinically trained leader. These groups seek to avoid the power differentials created when groups are conducted by individuals whose leadership is based on clinical training rather than survival of childhood sexual abuse. An example of a self-help group for survivors of childhood sexual abuse is Incest Survivors Anonymous, a 12-step programme based on the principles of Alcoholics Anonymous.

Such self-help programmes have the advantage of offering comradeship, support, understanding, recognition, and confrontation in groups that are easily accessible and often free of charge (Gil, 1990). In many cases, these groups provide a surrogate extended family. Self-help groups can, however, experience turbulence when intra-group conflict or power issues are not managed successfully, or when the group is unable to meet the safety needs of members with serious psychiatric symptoms (e.g. psychosis, suicidality).

Self-help groups typically do not use screening procedures (Gil, 1990). Continuity may also be a problem, as regular attendance is not required and group leadership may frequently change. Nonetheless, survivors who are in counselling may find involvement in self-help groups beneficial at some point in their healing process, especially when they are ready to withdraw from or supplement their counselling experience.

Clinical groups

The second type of survivor group is the professionally led group that is usually run in a mental health or social service agency. Several different formats can be used for clinical groups. They can be closed, structured, and time-limited (Bruckner and Johnson, 1987; Cole, 1985; Goodman and Nowak-Scibelli, 1985; Gordy, 1983; Herman and Schatzow, 1984; Tsai and Wagner, 1978), open, unstructured, and ongoing (Blake-White and Kline, 1985), or a combination of the two types (Harris, 1998; Sgroi, 1989b; Webb and Leehan, 1996). The advantages and disadvantages of each format will be outlined. Groups described in the literature that have been run according to each format will be discussed as examples.

SHORT-TERM, STRUCTURED GROUPS Short-term, structured groups typically have a limited number of sessions that are run according to a predetermined plan. Group membership is limited to those who enter the group at the beginning. These groups have also been referred to as programmatic groups (Briere, 1989).

There are several advantages to this group format. In closed groups, members all begin at the same time and are able to explore similar issues simultaneously, thereby enhancing group cohesiveness. Group activities and ground rules provide a structure to facilitate group development. Also, some survivors prefer to have a specified ending point as a parameter to the group experience. Shorter groups usually limit conflict between members, allowing them to focus specifically on the sexual abuse experience (Cole, 1985).

This type of group format also has several potential disadvantages. With a shorter time limit, some members may have difficulty feeling safe or developing a commitment to the group. Because the focus of each session is predetermined, members may feel as if they have little control over the course of the group. Also, if a closed group was started before a survivor decided to join, he or she would have to wait until a new group began. Once the survivor has decided to risk group involvement, it can be difficult to wait.

Cole (1985) described an incest survivor group led by a female therapist at a women's counselling centre. The group was conducted for six sessions, with each session lasting two hours. Each participant attended an intake session, at which time they were given literature related to sexual abuse to read prior to the start of the group. The goals and activities of each group session are outlined below.

Session 1. The focus of the first group session was to establish cohesion among group members and to encourage them to begin to discuss their incest experiences. Activities included introductory remarks by the therapist (e.g. acknowledgement of tension and anxiety, comments on common themes related to incest), an activity in which each participant interviewed another participant and introduced her partner to the group, beginning discussion of the incest experience by group members, specification of goals by each participant, and identification of one positive thing participants could do for themselves prior to the next group session.

Session 2. The goals of the second group session were to strengthen group cohesion and to specify or refine goals. Activities included processing members' reactions to the prior group session, a discussion of the incest literature that had been given out during the intake session, and the circulation of participants' names, addresses, and phone numbers to encourage out-of-group contact between members.

Session 3. Addressing issues of secrecy and isolation was the goal of the third group session. A discussion related to these issues was facilitated first in small groups and then in the larger group. The participants again were asked to identify something positive they could do for themselves during the following week.

Session 4. The goal of this group session was to address the issue of self-esteem and to provide the opportunity for participants to discuss their individual concerns. The participants brainstormed any phrases they associated with the word 'incest', and the leader wrote these phrases on a flip-chart. This was followed by a discussion. In addition, each participant was asked to say something positive about the survivor next to her.

Session 5. The goal of the fifth group session was to address the impact of the incest experience on group participants' current lives. Activities included a brainstorming session in which group participants listed children's rights (e.g. control over their bodies, non-sexual physical contact) and needs (e.g. affection, attention). In some of Cole's (1985) groups, members were asked to share with a partner a specific incest incident and then discuss their reactions to this experience with the whole group. The homework assignment was to complete a handout that addressed the stages of healing and included related questions for discussion.

Session 6. The goal of the sixth and final group session was the integration of information. Group members broke up into smaller groups to discuss the questions from the homework handout. Another goal was providing the opportunity for members to say goodbye. Each group member placed a large sheet of paper on the wall. All of the members then wrote positive goodbye messages on each person's paper. Further treatment options (e.g. individual counselling, assertiveness training) were discussed.

LONG-TERM, OPEN-ENDED GROUPS   A long-term, open-ended, unstructured group allows new members to join at any point, does not have a limited number of sessions, and generally does not have a predetermined structure for each group meeting. These groups have also been referred to as non-programmatic groups (Briere, 1989).

There are several advantages and disadvantages to this group format (Hall and Lloyd, 1989). With an open format, members typically have immediate access to the group and greater freedom to leave the group if it is not meeting their needs. New members can keep the group fresh and older members can provide support for newer members. As survivors repeatedly describe their experiences, the secrecy surrounding the abuse is lessened. Newer members may feel excluded in an open-ended group, however, and older members may be reluctant to continually share their experiences. Intra-group conflicts and breaches of confidentiality are more common. Joining a group without an identified ending point can be threatening for some survivors (Sgroi, 1989b).

Blake-White and Kline (1985) described an open-ended, long-term incest group conducted in a mental health centre. An open-ended group was chosen at this setting so that survivors could join when they were ready to do so, rather than waiting for a new group to begin. A long-term format was used, so that survivors could explore their issues in depth. There were no specified topics for each session, although participants were encouraged to describe their incest experiences. The group leaders described themselves as non-directive, but did indicate that they would encourage the group to focus on one or two issues a session. The leaders would assist members to reframe childhood misperceptions regarding the abuse, express feelings, and make connections between present behaviours and the abuse experience. Because members were at different stages in the healing process, the authors reported that newer members found hope in the progress of others and were able to accept confrontation from survivors who had 'been there'.

TIME-LIMITED, CONSECUTIVE GROUPS   Some group programmes combine elements of both the short-term and the long-term formats. Sgroi (1989b) described a series of time-limited survivor groups conducted by two female co-therapists at a private child abuse treatment centre. These groups are discussed here as an example of an alternative to either the strictly long-term or strictly short-term group formats.

Three groups were conducted at the centre each year, each running from 10 to 12 weeks. Survivors chose to participate in one, two, or all of the groups. A commitment to a time-limited group with an identified stopping point was experienced by some as less threatening, and more under their control, than an open-ended group. Having consecutively run groups also gave participants the option to continue with group treatment by joining another group cycle if they desired to do so.

A theme (e.g. dealing with fear, exercising control) was determined for each group. A screening process, based on several criteria (e.g. stabilization of acting-out behaviours, ability to discuss victimization experiences) was used. Co-therapist tasks include both attending to the personal treatment needs of each group member (e.g. identification of present coping mechanisms) and facilitating the group process. Group techniques included role playing, body sculpting, art therapy, hypnotic storytelling, and the use of metaphors.

TRAUMA RECOVERY GROUP   Harris and colleagues (1998) designed a 33-session group treatment programme for vulnerable women who have been traumatized. Although the group would be considered long-term, it is structured and close-ended. The treatment manual provides outlines of activities for the 33 graduated sessions, each of which focuses on a specific topic. Topics include empowerment (e.g. what it means to be a woman, physical and emotional boundaries, self-esteem, intimacy and trust), trauma recovery (e.g. understanding trauma, physical abuse, sexual abuse, emotional symptoms, addictive behaviours), advanced trauma recovery (e.g. family life; decision-making; communication; blame, acceptance, and forgiveness), and closing rituals (e.g. truths and myths about abuse, what it means to be a woman). The authors recommend that the sessions last 75 minutes. A clinical rationale, set of goals, series of questions to be posed to the group, and experiential exercise for each session are presented in the manual.

Issues involved in planning a survivor group

There are several issues for counsellors to consider when running a clinical group for survivors of childhood sexual abuse. These include: deciding on the number of sessions, choosing facilitators, determining group composition, and planning group time. Facilitators should also consider how to handle member screening issues, group ground rules, common group issues, and termination.

Determining the number of sessions

For a short-term structured group, facilitators need to determine how many sessions the group will run. This decision is based on group goals and available resources. While groups with few sessions (e.g. 6–8) are economical and facilitate a 'sharp focus on abuse-related issues' (Briere, 1989: 148), they provide limited opportunities for members to get acquainted with one another. This can prohibit in-depth discussion of issues. Longer-running groups (e.g. over 12 sessions) allow members to explore issues in more depth, to develop cohesion, and to work on abuse-related interpersonal problems (Briere, 1989: 148). Problems similar to those found in open-ended groups, however, may arise. Interpersonal conflicts, for example, may develop and interrupt the discussion of abuse-related concerns.

Counsellors who have run survivor groups have made recommendations regarding the optimal number of sessions for the short-term group. Cole stated:

> A six week model, an eight week model and a twelve week model were all tried. The six week model was the most used, due to availability of staff. However, the eight and twelve week models were preferable in giving the clients more opportunity for exploring issues. In the twelve week format transference issues were more apparent as was conflict between group members. (1985: 80)

Briere reached a similar conclusion:

> Although the optimal number of sessions may thus vary according to the goals of treatment, as well as the setting in which therapy is taking place, the author has found that 10 to 12 sessions (the average number cited in the abuse group literature) is often most effective – allowing enough time for group cohesion to occur, and yet not so extended that intra-group conflicts and habitually dysfunctional behaviours supersede abuse-related concerns. (1989: 148)

Choice of facilitators

Facilitators of survivor groups should have expertise in abuse issues and skills in group leadership. It is helpful to have at least two counsellors facilitate each group (Webb and Leehan, 1996). Survivor groups typically elicit painful material and intense affect; co-facilitators can provide support for one another and discuss the dynamics of the group following each session. Two facilitators can also share leadership tasks. For example, while one focuses on the needs of an individual group member, the other may attend to group process. Co-facilitators must develop trust and good communication with each other. Supervision is helpful to address issues that arise in the working relationship.

The gender mix of the co-facilitator team is another issue that has been discussed by counsellors who run survivor groups. Although some counsellors suggest that a mixed-gender co-facilitator team for a women's survivor group may have some advantages (e.g. providing opportunities for members to develop a healthy relationship with a male), two female facilitators may be more likely to enhance trust early in the group process.

Bruckner and Johnson discussed their recommendations regarding the optimal gender mix of the co-facilitator team for a male survivor group:

We found it difficult to choose the makeup of the co-facilitator team. From our work with women's support groups, we felt that two female facilitators or a mixed-gender team would be more effective. Based on participants' reports, a minority of women's group participants found it very difficult to disclose and reveal their feelings openly with a male facilitator present. No male participants reported heightened discomfort with a female present. However, they expressed interest in the female therapist's reaction to discussion about current sexual behaviours. They seemed to need her acceptance and permission. Based on our work with male groups, we feel that a female co-facilitator helps reduce discomfort while allowing participants to practice disclosure with both sexes. (1987: 87)

Group composition

Facilitators of survivor groups must determine the composition of group membership. For example, some groups limit membership to those individuals who have been sexually abused, whereas other groups may also include members who were physically or emotionally abused. Many counsellors believe that survivors of all types of abuse experience similar issues and profit from sharing their experiences with other survivors. Gil, who conducts such mixed groups, stated:

This [a mixed group] works well as long as there are an approximately equal number of victims of each type of abuse. The only mixed group that is difficult to conduct is one in which most of the clients were abused in one way, while one or two were abused in another way (for example, eight victims of incest and one victim of physical abuse). This tends to split the group. It also encourages the minority members to feel isolated, misunderstood, and undeserving of help. (1990: 204)

Because sexual abuse survivors have been subjected to activities that are especially taboo in our society and interfere significantly with psychosexual development, groups that include only survivors of childhood sexual abuse may be preferable for dealing specifically with issues of shame and sexuality. Also, feelings of isolation are probably best addressed in a group composed entirely of sexual abuse survivors.

Groups may include both male and female survivors or may be limited to one gender. Mixed-gender groups do have the advantage of helping survivors appreciate the universality of the victimization experience. Due to issues of trust and the divergent ways in which female and male survivors may express the abuse sequelae, however, separate gender groups may be preferable, at least for the initial group experience. Briere (1989) suggested that other mixes of clients (based on age, race, sexual orientation, diagnosis, etc.) will do well together in groups, although it may be important to balance some client traits (e.g. verbal versus less verbal members).

Planning group time

Regardless of the basic format of the group, facilitators will need to make decisions regarding how group time will be structured. Hall and Lloyd (1989) have identified three approaches to planning group time.

One approach is to introduce common topics or themes for discussion at the beginning of each session. This will serve to focus the group meetings and to increase survivors' sense of universality by demonstrating that others struggle with many of the same issues as they do. In structured groups, facilitators often identify these themes in advance. In unstructured groups, facilitators identify issues and themes that arise in group discussions and help the group focus on one of them. Examples of themes that might be discussed in groups include: responsibility for the abuse, the dynamics of the incestuous family, the prevalence of childhood sexual abuse in society, the impact of the abuse on members' current relationships, handling abuse-related effects (e.g. post-traumatic symptoms, guilt, low self-esteem), interacting with families of origin (e.g. whether or not to confront the offender or non-offending family members), planning ways to care for oneself, and moving on (e.g. forgiveness, finding meaning in the experience, giving up the survivor identity, helping others).

Planned group exercises, another approach to the use of group time, can serve several purposes. Activities can be focused on helping members address issues experientially, develop group cohesion, and practise skills. As discussed above, short-term, structured groups are often based on several exercises that are planned by facilitators prior to the beginning of the group. Open-ended, unstructured groups often incorporate such activities as group needs dictate. For example, if several members are having difficulty appreciating their 'childlikeness' at the time of the abuse, facilitators may introduce an exercise in which members are asked to bring in childhood photos. Some group activities that have been used in survivor groups include:

1   having group members draw pictures of their families, themselves as children, or the scene where the abuse took place to encourage the non-verbal expression of feelings and to facilitate feedback among group members (Hall and Lloyd, 1989);

2   planning a shared activity, often a common meal or a recreational activity (e.g. a visit to a museum), or engaging in a task requiring cooperation (e.g. designing an anti-abuse poster) to enhance group cohesion;

3   brainstorming (asking group members to spontaneously generate thoughts that are then written on a large sheet of paper) to facilitate discussion of certain themes or to create a sense of universality. For example, a group may brainstorm engagement strategies that offenders might use to gain victims' cooperation. This activity would address the responsibility issue of compliance (i.e., 'He didn't use force, so I must have wanted it');

4   listing strengths and weaknesses or negative self-perceptions that members hold about themselves. These lists are shared with the group and feedback is given to address self-esteem issues and cognitive distortions;

5   discussing literature that was read by all group members to facilitate discussion of specific themes (e.g. Herman's [1981] work on the three 'discoveries' of incest);

6   participating in skill-enhancement activities (e.g. assertiveness training, parent training, relaxation training) to address current abuse-related problems.

A third way group time may be used is giving each member an opportunity to discuss pertinent current concerns or past issues and to receive feedback from the group (Hall and Lloyd, 1989). Facilitators afford all members 'individual time' and monitor group members' responses to the individual who is speaking.

In addition to these approaches, facilitators often choose to discuss group process issues related to interpersonal events among members or between members and facilitators (e.g. conflict, dependency). Addressing these issues can facilitate smoother group functioning and assist members in dealing with the interpersonal issues that often bring them to the group initially.

Facilitators may utilize several different methods to begin and end group meetings. Sessions may be opened with a 'check-in' with each member to see how he or she is doing (Gil, 1990), a review of the last meeting, or a sharing of recent achievements (Hall and Lloyd, 1989). Similarly, each session may end with a 'check-in' to see if any member is feeling distressed or unsafe (Hall and Lloyd, 1989), a summary of the events of the group, or a confirmation of the agenda for the next meeting. Some facilitators also choose to give homework assignments, such as journal keeping or reading related to the aspect of childhood abuse that was discussed in the group session.

Screening

Potential group members should meet with facilitators prior to group involvement. During this meeting, the format, structure, and ground rules of the group can be described. The survivors' goals and the group's purpose are discussed to determine if the group can adequately meet the needs of the survivor.

Group facilitators often develop membership criteria. If survivors exhibit problems that limit their ability to participate fully in a group or that may result in disruption of the group, they are often referred for individual therapy or for other appropriate services (e.g. hospitalization, substance abuse treatment programmes). Exclusionary criteria may include: psychosis or disorientation; active suicidality; excessive hostility or aggressiveness; current abuse of drugs or alcohol; and an inability to discuss the abuse experience to any extent with the screener.

Briere (1989) cautioned facilitators against using strict exclusion criteria, some of which reflect typical long-term effects of abuse (i.e., suicidality). Using such criteria automatically eliminates many survivors who request group treatment. He suggested that facilitators evaluate the extent of each survivor's problem (e.g. distinguishing active suicidal intent from passing suicidal thoughts), and the degree to which these problems would actually interfere with group involvement.

Membership criteria are also often dependent on other factors, such as the setting in which the group is run. For example, some in-patient facilities provide intensive group therapy for survivors who are acutely suicidal because they can be closely monitored for any self-destructive behaviour that is exacerbated by group participation. Because community groups are unable to provide such support, they often screen out actively suicidal survivors.

The screening meeting can be used as a goal-setting session, in which facilitators can determine if the survivor's goals are appropriate for the format of the group. For example, sharing one's abuse experience with other survivors or receiving feedback from others regarding responsibility issues would be appropriate goals for a short-term group. Learning to trust others, however, is probably not a realistic goal to be achieved in 6–12 sessions. During the screening process, facilitators can either help survivors refine goals that cannot realistically be met by the group or refer them to a more appropriate group.

Ground rules and boundaries

Group facilitators must identify and discuss group ground rules (Webb and Leehan, 1996). Ground rules in most groups are related to confidentiality, safety, group time, attendance, and out-of-group contact.

CONFIDENTIALITY Because trust is a key issue in survivor groups, confidentiality is an important ground rule to address. Facilitators should state the expectation that no material discussed in the group will be shared outside the group. Facilitators should specify, however, that they cannot guarantee this and it is each member's responsibility to maintain confidentiality. If the facilitators share group material with colleagues for the purpose of consultation, supervision, or collaboration with individual therapists, group members should be informed of this. Members should also be told that some information will not be kept confidential (e.g. intent to harm self or others, child abuse).

SAFETY Ground rules related to safety issues should be addressed as well. Facilitators should emphasize that the physical safety of members must be respected and that no physical violence will be tolerated in the group. Ground rules regarding members' emotional safety can also be important. It is useful, for example, to discuss the differences between a personal verbal attack and helpful confrontation.

GROUP TIME Because survivors often struggle with boundary issues, group parameters, such as the starting and stopping times of the sessions, should be clearly specified and maintained. Groups can become emotionally charged as the designated stopping time approaches; in these instances it can be tempting to extend group time to obtain closure on issues that may have arisen late in the session. If such issues do arise, group facilitators should acknowledge the fact that the session is ending with unfinished business. Regularly extending group time to resolve issues represents a disrespect of the boundaries of the group members and facilitators. Instead, facilitators may assist the group in making plans for addressing unfinished issues in another way. For example, a group may agree to begin the next session with the unresolved issue or help members who are distressed at the end of a group session plan how they can take care of themselves or meet their safety needs until the group meets again.

ATTENDANCE   Expectations regarding group attendance should be addressed. While members of some support groups are not expected to attend all meetings, most clinical group facilitators request that members come regularly and contact the facilitator if they are unable to attend a session.

Facilitators of short-term groups typically ask members to commit to all sessions before beginning the group. Similarly, facilitators of long-term, open-ended groups often ask survivors to commit to a certain number of sessions (e.g. four) in order to give the group a 'fair try' (Webb and Leehan, 1996). This discourages survivors from fleeing after an initial session due to anxiety or shame related to exposure. If a survivor does choose to leave the group, however, this decision should be respected. Some facilitators may request that the survivor share with the group his or her reason for leaving. This helps to decrease other members' feelings of rejection or abandonment, and gives the departing group member a sense of closure.

OUT-OF-GROUP CONTACT   Contact between group sessions, both among members and between members and facilitators, is another issue to discuss with group members. Some group facilitators actively encourage group members to have contact with each other between sessions, as it is believed that this can decrease isolation (Cole, 1985; Webb and Leehan, 1996). There are some disadvantages to this practice. If survivors have not yet dealt with issues of personal boundaries, assertiveness, and limit setting, they can feel overwhelmed if another group member calls them in distress or begins to depend on them for support. The advantages and disadvantages of out-of-group contact should be addressed. Members should be encouraged to make their own choices regarding the sharing of phone numbers and addresses.

Out-of-group contact with facilitators is also an issue to address at the beginning of a group. Some facilitators believe that their availability between sessions enables survivors to feel safe and supported. Others discourage between-session contact to avoid having members deal individually with issues that are best discussed in the group. As out-of-group contacts can represent boundary issues, the facilitator's policy should be clearly defined. Regardless, plans should be made to meet group members' individual and emergency counselling needs as they arise during group involvement. This can be accomplished by requiring members to have continuing contact with an individual therapist or by providing access to a crisis service (e.g. a hotline, an emergency service facility).

Common group issues

Several common issues that arise in survivor groups require leader intervention. Although any number of approaches can be used when these issues arise, some suggested counsellor interventions are outlined below.

Resistance

As the issue of childhood sexual abuse can be very difficult to share with others, group members often exhibit resistance to group participation. Anxiety precipitated by the group experience can cause members to miss sessions, come late to sessions, or forget to complete homework assignments. Counsellor interventions that may be used to address behaviours related to resistance include the following:

1 Confront the behaviour (e.g. absence from sessions) in a non-judgmental manner.
2 Encourage resistant survivors to describe their group experiences (e.g. what it was like for them to disclose the abuse) in order to begin to identify their anxiety.
3 Respond empathically to the emotional distress of the survivor.
4 Assist the survivor in connecting the resistant behaviour with his or her anxiety.
5 Ask other group members to give feedback to the resistant member regarding how they are affected by his or her behaviour and to share their ways of handling the anxiety they experience as a group member.

In the following interaction, both group members and the facilitator confront a survivor's resistance, which was evidenced by her missing several sessions following the disclosure of her abuse experience.

Counsellor: Polly, I've noticed you've missed the last two sessions.
Jane: Ya, where have you been, Polly?
June: Yes, everyone was asking about you.
Jane: We missed you.
June: You agreed to come to all the sessions.
Gretchen: Last time you were here you were so upset. We worried about you.
Polly: Really, it's no big deal, OK. I'll come from now on. For heaven's sake, I'm OK.
Counsellor: What is it like to hear that other group members missed you and were concerned about you?

Polly: I was afraid everyone would make a fuss like this. I was embarrassed the last time I was here. I never cry like that. I shouldn't have said what I did about my father. I really didn't want everyone worrying about me.

Counsellor: It was not only hard, then, for you to disclose your abuse and to experience the feelings that resulted from that, but it was also hard to have others show caring and concern for you.

Polly: Well, I'm certainly not used to it. My husband couldn't have cared less when I told him about what happened to me. You'd think I'd like people fussing about me, but it makes me uncomfortable.

Counsellor: Has anyone else experienced anything similar to this?

Jane: Yes, I missed a lot of group sessions at first too. It was hard to face everyone. I just stayed away. Now, I never miss.

Counsellor: What is different for you now?

Jane: I think I just feel more comfortable here. Polly will too if she just sticks it out. You have to force yourself to come. Then you learn everyone really means well.

Counsellor: Yes, sharing experiences and feelings is not easy, especially when you are used to others ignoring those feelings. As you have pointed out, Jane, you missed sessions rather than face sharing with the group.

Jane: Ya, but you have to hang in there.

Polly: I'll try. That's why I am here tonight.

Silence

Some members attend group regularly but consistently remain silent. When this occurs, counselling interventions may include the following:

1   Confront the silence in a non-judgmental manner.
2   Ask silent group members to describe their group experiences.
3   Help silent group members to connect their silence to anxiety, problems with trust, or low self-esteem (i.e., their feeling that what they have to say is not valuable, or even that it is stupid).
4   Ask other members to share any reluctance they have had speaking in group.
5   Encourage silent members to slowly begin to risk sharing their experiences and reactions with the group.

In the following interaction, a group member's silence is addressed:

Janice: You know, April, it's been three weeks and you haven't said a word. I wonder what you are thinking sometimes.

April: I really haven't had anything to say.

Janice: Everyone else said something about guilt [that day's topic].

April: I'll try to come up with something next time. I really can't think of anything right now. Sorry.

Counsellor: Sometimes it's hard to speak up in group. Has anyone else had problems at any point sharing their thoughts or feelings here?

Dodie: I did at first. I thought everyone would laugh at me.

Susan: Me, too. It seemed like everyone knew each other and said all these insightful things.

Joan: I was used to everyone, you know, my family, telling me to shut up. I came here and I'm supposed to speak up?

Dodie: That's it. We're used to keeping secrets. Here we tell really private things. It's hard.

Counsellor: So there are many reasons why it's hard to talk here. You may fear others will laugh or think you are stupid. You may have gotten the message from others outside of the group to be quiet or to keep secrets. Are any of these things similar to what you've experienced, April?

April: Yes, the sounding stupid part.

Joan: Believe me, you won't sound stupid. We've all gone through similar stuff. We won't laugh at you.

April: I never spoke up in school, either. I was dumb there.

Joan: Me too. But group is different. When you're ready, we would like to hear from you.

Hostility

As safety issues are paramount in survivor groups, hostility expressed by group members is a particularly important issue to address. When anger is expressed in a destructive way toward group members (e.g. threats, verbal abuse, name calling), facilitators should help restore an atmosphere of support. Counsellors may use the following interventions:

1 Clearly define unacceptable hostile behaviours and restrict these behaviours in group.
2 Discuss the difference between hostility, which is distancing in relationships, and the constructive expression of anger, which can enhance relationships.
3 Facilitate the appropriate expression of anger.
4 Ask other group members to describe their responses to the hostile behaviour and the ways they handle their own anger in the group.

In the following interaction, one group member's hostility to another is addressed:

Susy: Don't tell me that you understand what I feel. I'm sick to death of your garbage. Always having an opinion about my life when your life is such a mess. Frankly, I wish you would stop being a busybody or a shrink and leave me alone.

Jacqueline: Sorry, I was just trying to help.

Counsellor: Susy, one ground rule we have established in this group is that no one can verbally attack anyone else. If you are angry at Jacqueline, you can tell her that, but you cannot call her names or ridicule her ideas or her feedback.

Susy: She's always on my case and I'm sick of it.

Counsellor: Would you tell Jacqueline how you feel and what you would like from her without putting her down?

Susy: All right. All right. I get angry when you tell me what to do all the time. I will leave my husband when I'm ready. Just listen to me. Don't give me advice.

Monopolizing the group

Some members may tend to monopolize the group. One example of this is the group member who has multiple problems that he or she brings to group each week. Counselling interventions to address this issue include the following:

1   Confront the behaviour in a non-judgmental manner.
2   Set limits on the behaviour.
3   Support other members in providing constructive feedback.
4   Assist the survivor in connecting his or her behaviour with anxiety, problems with boundaries and control, or a need for attention (Gil, 1990).
5   Facilitate a group discussion regarding how to meet needs for attention in ways that do not distance others.

In the following interaction, Jim, a group member who tends to monopolize the group, is confronted by other group members and the group leader.

Jim: I would like to discuss a fight I had with my wife. You see, I was late coming home on Wednesday . . .

Peter: Come on, Jim. All last week we talked about you and your wife. Jeff, here, confronted his brother [the offender] and we haven't even heard how that went.

Jim: Sorry, I thought we were supposed to say what's on our minds. Go ahead, Jeff. I won't say another word.

Counsellor: Let's talk about what happened between Jim and Peter, and then I know I would like to hear from Jeff as well. What was Peter's feedback like for you, Jim?

Jim: Well, I know I talk a lot. I didn't like to hear it, though. I was a little angry. I think anyone would be. I guess I know I turn others off sometimes.

Counsellor: Peter, what was it like for you to give the feedback?

Peter: I didn't want to hurt his feelings, but I think we should all have more time to talk. It was hard to be the one to say something.

Counsellor: So it was hard for you to say and hard for Jim to hear. And yet we are here to give and receive feedback. Let's talk about how we use air time in the group. Usually, members who use a lot of air time are needing something from the group. Jim, could you talk about what you might need from the group now?

Jim: I guess this is the only place people listen to me. My wife doesn't, my family doesn't.

Counsellor: How might you meet your need to be heard in this group without using too much 'air time,' which, as you say, can turn others off?

Termination

Regardless of the format of the group, termination is always a significant issue. In structured groups, activities are often planned to help survivors review their group experiences, say goodbye to other members, deal with their feelings of loss, and plan future courses of action. In open-ended groups, the issues are dealt with as each individual chooses to end his or her involvement with the group.

Briere (1989) identified three important principles related to termination in survivor groups. First, the termination date is specified well in advance of the final meeting. Second, group members are frequently reminded that group participation, even if it is long term, is for a finite period. This allows all members to prepare for termination throughout their group experience. Lastly, the final group sessions should be ceremonialized, so that survivors have the opportunity to experience closure and say goodbye.

In the following interaction, the group facilitator encourages group members to deal with their feelings of loss. The interaction takes place following a party that members had planned for the final session of a 12-week survivor group.

Sharon: Well, this is over. It really wasn't so bad. I thought I would hate coming and then I ended up looking forward to it.

Counsellor: What about the group will you miss?

Sharon: Just coming here, having someone to talk to. I never told anyone what was done to me. I'll miss this group on Tuesday nights.

Counsellor: Does anyone else have similar feelings?

June: I do. It's like I just got to know everyone and now I will not see you all any more.

Darlene: I felt kind of sad coming tonight. I almost stayed home.

Tanya: I wonder what I will do with myself on Tuesdays. I feel like you are my friends. I know some of us will keep in touch, but not everyone. You know, we say we will meet for coffee but we probably won't.

Counsellor: So it is important to say goodbye tonight.

Tanya: Yes. You know you tell people you'll see them around and you know you won't.

Counsellor: Saying 'I'll see you later' is really a way to avoid saying goodbye, which can be very hard.

Tanya: Now you're going to make me cry. I've only known you all a few months and yet I've never felt closer to any other women.

Terry: I think it's because we all went through something similar.

Darlene: Yes, many of my friends know I was abused, but this is different. They really don't understand like you all did.

Counsellor: So you will be saying goodbye tonight to others to whom you feel very close to in a special way. Are there particular things you would like to say to each other?

Tanya: I want to tell Terry I appreciated the time she held my hand when I was crying about my mother leaving me . . .

10

Case Study: The Counselling Process with an Adult Survivor of Childhood Sexual Abuse

This chapter illustrates counselling principles by describing the counselling experience of Sue, an adult survivor of childhood sexual abuse who sought counselling at a community agency. Sue was in individual counselling for approximately a year and a half. This was her first counselling experience.

Background

Sue was a 44-year-old woman who sought counselling for complaints of general life dissatisfaction and concern about her drinking habits. Because she broke several scheduled appointments, she did not come for an intake session for several months after her initial call to the agency. She claimed that she had cancelled the appointments to take her mother to various doctor's appointments.

When Sue finally did attend a scheduled appointment, she told the counsellor that she was very anxious. She stated, 'I never thought I would be the type of person to do this [seek counselling].' She began by describing herself as a 'plain Jane old maid'. Sue revealed that she got up one morning and realized that she was unhappy with her life and did not want to 'live the next 20 years like I lived that last 20'. However, she was unable to articulate what changes she wanted to make in her life other than to 'get out more with people'. She did report that she had completely stopped drinking over two months before, when she made the initial call for a counselling appointment.

An assessment revealed that Sue was living with her 76-year-old mother, who was in poor health due to long-standing heart problems. Sue reported that she had been taking care of her mother for many years by doing her shopping and housekeeping and making her doctor's appointments. She described their relationship as strained and conflict-ridden. She claimed her mother was very 'cranky' and would usually complain that Sue was not doing things right. At times, Sue resented that fact that her mother depended on her so much. Sue's father and mother had been separated for approximately 33 years. Her father lived in a distant state. Sue would call him periodically, but he would usually be drunk when she called.

Sue had two older sisters and one younger brother. Her sisters were both married and living in another state. They visited infrequently, usually during the holidays. Sue stated that her younger brother, John, had emotional problems and was currently living in a nearby rooming house. When he ran out of money, he would sometimes return to live with Sue and her mother. Sue said this arrangement was problematic as John was 'difficult to control' and at times would become violent when angry. Although he did not attack Sue or her mother, he would destroy their belongings (e.g. smash dishes, break furniture). Sue stated that he would also get drunk, steal from the family, and stay away for days at a time. Sue's mother would insist that Sue 'keep an eye' on John when he stayed with them.

Sue was employed as the receptionist and secretary for a small local industry. She had been at her job for over 26 years, since graduating from high school. Although she was reluctant to compliment herself, Sue indicated that her work was highly regarded by her employer. She had not missed a day of work since she was hired. Although her work could be monotonous at times, she basically enjoyed her job and her relationship with co-workers.

After work, Sue would usually stop at a local restaurant for dinner and a few drinks. She would then come home to watch television and have a few more drinks. She stated that she had no friends outside of work other than Jim, a young man who lived in the apartment above hers. She described him as a 'shy loner – much like me'. Jim would suggest from time to time that they get married, but Sue denied any interest in Jim that was 'more than friends'. Sue reported that she had always been isolated from anyone outside her family.

Sue was somewhat vague when answering questions about her childhood. She denied any abuse, although she did claim that her father was 'very strict' with the other children – 'whipping them when they needed it'. She 'got off the hook' because she never got into any trouble. Her dad 'drank too much sometimes' and 'had quite the temper'. Sue described her family as very conservative and religious. She stated that they had few friends outside of the church. Sue's mother was often sick. Sue laughed, 'I guess things haven't changed much – I was calling the doctor for her even back then.'

Sue remained somewhat hesitant about counselling, but stated, 'I'm depressed, lonely, and bored and need to do something.' Sue and the counsellor agreed to work on Sue's social relationships and her conflicted relationship with her mother.

Disclosing an experience of childhood sexual abuse

During the second session, Sue appeared very anxious and avoided eye contact with the counsellor. She began the session by stating, 'I think I had better tell you about some weird dreams I've been having.' Sue revealed that she had had several dreams in which she is a little girl and a 'shadowy figure' climbs into bed with her. Sometimes this figure would have a knife or a spear. She experienced these dreams as very frightening. She feared that having these 'dirty' dreams meant that she was 'some kind of pervert'. In the following interaction, Sue discusses the dreams and reveals that she was sexually abused by her father as a child.

> *Sue*: I think it's strange I would have such a weird dream. It is so bizarre. I must be some kind of weirdo. I wasn't just in bed with him. It was like, well, sexual. It's like the figure touches me, in my private parts. The dreams are fuzzy, I cannot remember everything.
> *Counsellor*: What do the dreams mean to you?
> *Sue*: It's just bizarre. I know people have weird dreams, but this is too strange. You must think I'm perverted.
> *Counsellor*: No, I don't. People can have dreams like this for any number of reasons. I can see it was hard for you to tell me about these dreams, however, and I respect your courage for bringing them up.
> *Sue*: Maybe I should tell you. I wasn't completely honest with you last time. [*Long pause*] I think it happened in real life. My father did stuff to me. I do not remember all the details, but I do know he would come to my bed and would, you know, fondle me. That I do remember. This is probably hard for you to believe. For a long time I pretended it did not happen. I'm embarrassed to tell you. This is not why I am here. It's not important. It is my mother who drives me crazy, not my father.
> *Counsellor*: I can appreciate that it was hard for you to tell me about this. I am glad you chose to share this. We may decide to explore these childhood experiences and see how they may be related to the concerns you have now.

Upon further questioning, Sue revealed that her father had fondled her in her bed about once a week for a period of two years, starting when Susan was about eight. It usually occurred when he was drunk and her mother was asleep. He convinced her never to tell her mother, by telling Susan that she was his 'special girl'. The nightmares began when she stopped drinking.

Discussion

Sue's initial presentation was consistent with a possible undisclosed history of sexual abuse. She presented with issues common to sexual abuse survivors: social isolation, substance abuse, and being in a caretaking role that she clearly resented. In addition, she also described a history of parentification in which she had cared for a sickly mother from a young age. The family was isolated and her father was impulsive, violent, and chemically dependent. Sue indicated that her other siblings had been beaten by their father, but she was vague when asked about her own treatment by him. While the counsellor did not suggest that trauma was a factor related to Sue's current concerns, she did formulate an index of suspicion.

During the second session, Sue disclosed a possible trauma-related symptom, an ongoing intrusive nightmare. When the counsellor assured Sue that she did not consider her 'perverted' because of her dreams, Sue disclosed long-term sexual abuse by her father. The counsellor responded to this disclosure with calm concern, and suggested they explore the significance of this abuse in Sue's life.

Focusing on the abuse experience

The counselling agreement

Sue at first denied that the sexual abuse by her father was a significant childhood event related to her current concerns. After a few sessions, however, the nightmare of the 'shadowy figure' became more frequent and more violent in content. Sue described waking up just as the figure was about to stab her. She decided to focus on the abuse experience after the following interaction with her counsellor:

> Sue: I'm 44. I'm lonely. I've stopped drinking and yet I'm still miserable. Now, on top of this, I've been thinking about my dad as a dirty old man who messed with me. Bringing this up has not helped me. In fact, it's made me more depressed. I still have the problem I came here with. I'm alone and I don't know what to do about it. The abuse happened, but so what?

Counsellor: An abuse experience like the one you suffered as a child may be related in some way to the struggles you have now.

Sue: How can this be? As nearly as I can figure out, it happened almost 36 years ago.

Counsellor: Being sexually abused as a young child by a parent can affect how the child relates to others when he or she grows up. Or – the way the child learns to cope with the abuse continues to be the way he or she copes with things as an adult.

Sue: Like – I always hid out in my room as a kid. Now I know I was probably trying to get away from what was happening. I played alone for hours and had no friends. I still hide out in my room now in a way. Instead of Barbie dolls, I leaned on my bourbon. I still have no friends. Maybe my messed-up childhood does have something to do with all this. How will talking about it help, though?

Discussion

In this interaction, the counsellor explored a possible connection between the abuse and Sue's current difficulties. For Sue, making the connection between hiding out in her room as a child and 'hiding out' as an adult was a powerful experience. If she had not made a connection between the abuse and her current concerns, she probably would not have chosen to continue to deal with the abuse issue in counselling. At this point, the counsellor described the purpose of the exploratory work (e.g. translation of memories into a narrative, making sense of her life story, experiencing emotions at a pace that is safe and manageable) and answered questions Sue had about the abuse-focused approach to counselling. Because Sue had made a connection between her past and present, and thereby ceased to minimize the abuse, she contracted with the counsellor to focus on the abuse experience as a way of better understanding her current difficulties.

Preparing for exploratory work

Both Sue and the counsellor were concerned about Sue's drinking history. Sue readily agreed that her drinking was one way she had coped with the pain in her life and her feelings of loneliness and boredom. Although she was proud that she had stopped drinking on her own, she realized that she might be tempted to drink once she began to explore the abuse. She agreed to attend AA, both to address her abuse of alcohol and to decrease her social isolation. In time, she became an avid AA member.

Sue and the counsellor also discussed the relationship between Sue's nightmares and the abuse. The counsellor informed Sue that the nightmares might become more troubling as they began to explore the abuse in greater depth. Together they planned how Sue could manage the nightmares if this occurred. Sue placed an award that she had received at work as 'Employee of the Year' on her nightstand. When awakened by a nightmare, she would reach out for this plaque and it would ground her to present reality. This associational cue worked particularly well as it clearly reflected Sue's competency as an adult.

For Sue, the preparatory period was brief. She had been sober for several months and was functioning relatively well. Some experts may argue for a longer period of sobriety before exploring the abuse in depth. The counsellor felt that Sue was ready to begin the exploratory work after about four sessions. Although Sue had been reluctant to discuss the abuse when she first came to counselling, once she decided that exploring this issue would help she was determined to get started.

Exploratory work

Several approaches were used to help Sue explore her abuse. She remembered many abuse incidents but was 'fuzzy' about the details. Discussing general childhood events provoked more detailed memories of the abuse. For example, when Sue talked about her mother's preoccupation with health issues, the counsellor inquired as to what impact this had on Sue as a child. Sue revealed that her mother had taken her to the doctor for even the most minor ailments. During one visit, the doctor told her mother that Sue must have fallen off her bike as she had injuries 'down there'. At the time, Sue felt confused about this because she had not had any such accident. She remembered being concerned that her mother might have thought that she had sex at school, but her mother never mentioned the doctor's comments again. Looking back, Sue concluded that the vaginal injuries were probably the result of the sexual abuse, and that her mother did not respond to the doctor's revelation because she did not want to deal with what Sue's father had done. As Sue discussed this incident, memories of some abuse incidents became clearer and she recalled incidents of penetration as well as fondling.

Sue began to discuss the abuse incidents in some detail, but complained of feeling numb and 'distant from' the memories. The counsellor recommended that Sue bring in an old family photograph taken at a time when she was eight years old. Sue found only one old photo of her family. In the photo, she was eight years old. Sue asked her mother if there were other photos and her mother told her that the family had never owned a camera and that the photograph Sue had found was taken by her grand-mother. The photograph provoked several fruitful discussions about Sue's family. While viewing the photo, Sue discussed her father's alcoholism and his severe physical abuse of her brother, much of which Sue had witnessed. She also revealed that her mother did not seem to notice her brother's beatings. When discussing these family dynamics, Sue began to have an emotional response to her memories:

Sue: You know you can tell something is wrong with this family even by looking at this photo. No one is smiling. You know how families always smile in pictures. We all look miserable. No wonder we never had our own camera. Look at my brother. He looks mad! No wonder. My father beats him and my mother couldn't care less.
Counsellor: What do you think when you look at yourself in the picture?
Sue: I look dumb, I think. We all look weird. Other families stand close to each other or touch each other. We look wooden. My father even looks mean; my mother looks frail; I look spaced out.
Counsellor: Spaced out?
Sue: Ya, like not there. I have such a blank look.
Counsellor: What do you make of that?
Sue: It's like I checked out. I don't look happy. I don't look sad. I just look there. That's how I felt. I was just there. I don't remember being happy, but I don't remember being sad either. When my father beat my brother, I think I would kind of pretend that it wasn't happening. Like I made myself numb.
Counsellor: What do you think of when you look at your family as a whole?
Sue: Looking at this picture I realize this family is not normal. My father did what he wanted, my mother didn't notice, and I was spaced out. Like I was in a coma. [*She begins to cry softly.*] What a waste of a childhood.

Through discussions about her family's functioning, Sue concluded that her sisters, who both left home immediately after high school, might have been sexually abused. Her father had been extremely strict with her oldest sister, flying into a rage whenever she brought dates home. Sue, who by this time had read a good deal of material on incestuous families, concluded that her father's response to her sister's dates reflected a 'possessive jealousy', which is often characteristic of a sexually abusive father.

Sue decided to call her sisters and ask if they had been sexually abused by their father. The counsellor requested that they first spend time discussing Sue's plans (e.g. her motives, possible risks and benefits for both herself and her sisters). After these discussions, Sue remained determined to contact her sisters. She first called Jill, the younger of the two sisters, who denied abuse by her father and was quite critical that Sue should even suggest such a 'dirty-minded' thing. Despite having previously considered that this might be Jill's response, Sue nonetheless felt devastated at her sister's reaction to her disclosure and request for help. (It was later revealed by Sue's mother that all the girls had been sexually abused by their father.)

Sue's older sister Paula responded quite differently. When Sue told her the purpose of the call, Paula became very quiet and started to cry. Paula revealed that she had been abused by their father from the ages of 10 to 16, when she left home. She stated that she had hoped that Sue had been spared his abuse, but she had always wondered. Paula decided to visit Sue, and Sue invited her to one of the counselling sessions. Both sisters were very supportive of one another. They cried together and commiserated that although they had both suffered, until now they had not been able to share each other's pain.

Discussion

While Sue had some initial amnesia about the details of the abuse incidents (e.g. the vaginal penetration), these memories returned spontaneously through free narrative recall as she described other childhood experiences. Even when she began to discuss abuse incidents, she maintained good control over her intrusive nightmares and remained sober. However, she complained of being 'stuck' – i.e., having little emotional response to the discussions of the abuse. This is an example of defensive dissociation, in which memories are disconnected from overwhelming affect. The counsellor felt that they were 'undershooting' the therapeutic window as Sue continued to employ avoidant defences and was therefore describing, but not processing, the traumatic material. The counsellor decided to increase the use of exploratory interventions.

Several techniques were used, including viewing old photographs and processing Sue's interactions with her sisters. Although the counsellor did not recommend that Sue contact her sisters, she did acknowledge Sue's desire to do so and stressed the importance of first discussing the risks and benefits for all concerned. With the support of the counsellor and her older sister, Sue did begin to experience first sadness, then rage, toward her father. Although it was difficult to have these feelings, she claimed that she began to feel 'alive'. As she continued to discuss the abuse and her feelings regarding it, her nightmares began to subside. She remained sober throughout the process.

Reinterpreting the sexual abuse experience from an adult perspective

Because her father abused all his children, either sexually or physically, Sue blamed her father, not herself, for the abuse relatively early in her healing process. She did not struggle as intensely with responsibility issues as do some survivors. Following her interactions with her sisters, Sue quite clearly stated her belief that her father was a 'very sick man' and that she and her siblings were not to blame for the abuse.

She did deal, however, with the issue of sexual responsiveness. In her dream, she responded sexually to the shadowy figure. Sue asked, 'I know I was too young to ask for it [the abuse], but did I enjoy it?' When her sexual response was reframed by the counsellor as a natural physiological reaction, rather than an indication that she had enjoyed the activity, Sue was able to resolve this issue.

Addressing the context of the sexual abuse

Addressing the context of the sexual abuse experience was an important issue for Sue. In addition to the sexual abuse, her father's alcoholism and explosive temper and her mother's illnesses, obsession with the physical health of the family, and denial of the family violence had a significant impact on Sue's childhood development. Sue avidly read anything she could get her hands on regarding sexual abuse and alcoholic families. She identified herself as the 'family hero' (Wegscheider-Cruse, 1985), because she was always the child who did well at school and who had assumed the responsibility of caring for her mother. Sue was able to see how she continued to play these roles as an adult by being extremely responsible at work (e.g. never missing a day, 'doing the work of two people') and providing for her mother's, and now her brother's, needs. She recognized that she was unable to meet her own needs and, thus, had ultimately become very dissatisfied with her life.

Sue was especially interested in the concept of the closed family system (Satir, 1988). Her family's isolation had been profound. Her parents never socialized with others and discouraged the children from having friends. Sue recognized that Paula's attempts at dating, in addition to making her father jealous, had broken an unspoken family rule against interacting with outsiders. For this offence, Paula had been punished with her father's rage. Other attempts by the parents to discourage the children from having friends were more subtle. Often her parents would simply 'badmouth' other children with whom Sue or her siblings became friendly. Sue recognized that her isolation as an adult resulted in part from this deep distrust of those outside the family. Exploring her mother's role in the abuse was also important to Sue. While she acknowledged the rage she felt toward her father, she stated that she did not know how to feel toward her mother. After discussing her mother's behavior during Sue's childhood (e.g. pretending not to notice John's beatings; ignoring the doctor's revelation of Sue's 'accident'), Sue concluded that her mother knew something of the abuse, but did not intervene. In the following counsellor–client interaction, Sue reaches this conclusion and decides to discuss her suspicions with her mother. The counsellor again recommends that Sue plan for this confrontation before carrying it out.

> *Sue*: I can't believe she let this happen. But she must have. She never left the house. How could she not know? When the doctor told her about my 'accident', she never asked about it again. She must have known what really caused it or she would have asked me about it. Yes, she knew. She just ignored it.
>
> *Counsellor*: What has it been like for you to reach this conclusion about your mom?
>
> *Sue*: I don't know. I need to know for sure. Now, I can't feel anything. I mean if I really knew I would be angry. I need to ask her. After everything I've done for her. I was the only one to stick by her. I'm going to ask her when I get home.
>
> *Counsellor*: I can see it's important for you to find out whether your mother knew what your father was doing, and asking your mom directly would, of course, be a way to find out. It would be helpful to plan this ahead – what you will say to your mom, what you hope will happen, what it might feel like for you to do this, what effect it would have on her. That way it feels more in your control.
>
> *Sue*: OK, I won't run home and do it tonight.
>
> *Counsellor*: Let's start by discussing what it might be like for you to confront your mom.

Sue recognized that the confrontation in itself would be very difficult for her. She was accustomed to protecting her mom from anything unpleasant and, in this instance, she would be bringing up a painful issue. She hoped that her mom would confirm what Sue really believed to be true – i.e., that her mom knew of the abuse, but felt powerless to stop it. Sue knew this would be very hard to hear but would be a 'step in the right direction' toward sorting out her feelings regarding her mother's involvement in the abuse dynamics. Sue also explored her possible reactions if her mother denied knowledge of the abuse. She guessed that if her mother did not 'take responsibility and admit the truth', she would feel very resentful.

Before confronting her mom, Sue practised exactly what she wanted to say. She decided to begin the conversation with this statement, 'Mom, I now know Dad abused me by having sex with me when I was little. I do not question that it happened. Would you tell me if you were aware he was doing this to me? It is important to me that I know.'

When Sue confronted her mother, her mother did admit that she had known what the father was doing to all the kids (i.e., sexually abusing the girls and physically abusing John). Sue's mother confirmed Sue's belief that she felt powerless to stop the abuse because of her husband's violent temper, the family's dependency on his paycheck, and her own ill-health. Sue's mother became very tearful and yet 'somehow calm' as she said that she had hoped that Sue had been too young to realize what was happening to her. Her mother told Sue that one of the reasons her father had left the house when he did was because he was afraid Paula would tell the authorities of her abuse.

Sue initially felt enraged with her mother. She became very resentful that she had been her mom's caretaker all these years, whereas her mom had not protected her when she was a young child. Eventually, Sue came to appreciate her mother's limitations, which Sue called her 'extreme weakness of character'. Sue stated that she did not forgive her mother for not protecting her from the abuse. She did, however, resolve her own feelings toward her mother by coming to understand why she had not taken action. She was, therefore, no longer consumed with needing to know what her mother knew about the abuse and felt less bitterness as time went on.

Sue began to identify the unhealthy aspects of their relationship and decided to make changes in the way she interacted with her mother. She realized, for example, that many of the things she did for her mother (e.g. arranging doctor's appointments) were things her mother could do for herself. Ultimately, despite protests from her mother, Sue decided to move to her own apartment and gradually gave up much of the caretaking role. She also set limits on John's behaviours, although she continued to bail him out of trouble from time to time.

Discussion

Counselling interventions that were aimed at helping Sue explore the context of the abuse included facilitating a discussion related to dysfunctional families. When Sue recognized that she had assumed the role of the responsible, but joyless, child in her family and that the family system in which she grew up was extremely closed, she came to appreciate that her social isolation, her main presenting concern, was in many ways an extension of her family's history. Having this insight freed her to make other choices regarding social relationships as an adult.

Sue needed to explore her mother's role in the abuse dynamics. As with Sue's sisters, the counsellor did not advise a confrontation. Once Sue had chosen this course of action, however, the counsellor did help her plan and process the experience. Sue confirmed what she had suspected about the extent of her mother's knowledge of the abuse and dealt with her feelings related to this. She was then able to decide what kind of relationship she would like to maintain with her mother.

Making desired life changes

Even prior to beginning counselling, Sue had made a major life change: achieving and maintaining sobriety. However, she continued to feel lonely and isolated, often seeing only her mother, her brother John, and a few co-workers during the course of a day. As previously mentioned, she realized that she was continuing a family pattern of social isolation. Sue also recognized that the abuse and the family dynamics that surrounded it had made her feel poorly about herself, believing she would have very little to offer if she did make any friends. She continued to complain, 'I'm a plain Jane old maid.' In the following client–counsellor interaction, this self-perception was challenged.

> *Sue*: I look at other people, you know, married people. Or people having fun, going on dates. I'm so plain, so boring. The original old maid.
>
> *Counsellor*: I've noticed that you often refer to yourself as a 'plain old maid'. Tell me who first told you in some way that you were plain.
>
> *Sue*: Who first told me? Well, it must have been my parents, of course. I've always been ugly, even as a child. My father called me an 'ugly duckling'. I didn't mind. I was a tomboy, unlike Paula who was really pretty.
>
> *Counsellor*: So, your mom and dad first gave you the message that you were plain?
>
> *Sue*: Yes. I guess being plain looking actually saved me some of the pain Paula went through. I told you what happened because she had dates. You know, I remember my mother going through the ceiling when she came home one day with make-up. My father also went wild. I remember him scrubbing it off her face.
>
> *Counsellor*: What do you make of that now, looking back?

Sue: Well, it fits in with what we've been talking about. Being attractive or wearing make-up gets you noticed. Our parents didn't want us noticed.

Counsellor: Being a 'plain Jane' was what your family wanted you to be. It was what they expected.

Sue: Yes, but I am plain. Plain and dumpy. I did let myself get dumpy. My mother used to say heavy girls are virtuous, and 'shapely' girls are sluts. Jim tells me that I have nice eyes. That's what they tell fat people, nice eyes.

Counsellor: In your family you were expected to be plain and that's how you learned to see yourself. You tried to live up to those expectations, maybe by gaining weight. Yet those outside your family, like Jim, have seen something different, like your attractive eyes.

Sue: I can see where this is leading. I can make choices about how I look as an adult. I don't need to meet my parents' expectations. I'm not sure I believe that, but maybe I could spruce up a bit. I've lost weight since I stopped drinking and it does feel good. You also think I have nice eyes? [*laughs*]

A similar interaction addressed Sue's perception of herself as boring. In fact, she revealed that some of her co-workers liked to talk with her at lunch because she was so well read and kept up an interesting conversation. Also, Sue had a real sense of determination, which was probably what allowed her to stop drinking and deal with the sexual abuse issue so doggedly. Through discussions in counselling she became aware of this trait, an aspect of her personality to which she had never given credence. Exploring these strengths was a fruitful endeavour for Sue.

Having made progress in dealing with self-esteem issues, Sue then focused on her interpersonal relationships, the main issue that brought her to counselling. She decided that risking hurt was worth being less lonely. She joined an active, reputable singles' club – a major step for her. Attending the first few planned activities was very difficult for Sue, but she soon began to get to know several of the members, both male and female. Within a month of joining the club, she was asked out on a date. She began to see one of the members, Jake, on a regular basis. She eventually decided to end the relationship, realizing Jake had a 'drinking problem' and had begun to push for a sexual relationship that Sue did not want. Although she was disappointed that the relationship ended, she was well entrenched in the club and felt confident that she would meet someone else.

Discussion

Making life changes was an important aspect of Sue's healing. Stopping drinking, feeling better about herself, and becoming more active socially were all significant changes for her. Counselling interventions that challenged Sue's negative self-views and facilitated her increased awareness of her positive self-views were used to address self-esteem issues. Supportive interventions, such as encouraging Sue to discuss her new activities, were helpful as she risked new social interactions. In this phase of counselling, Sue expressed her belief that 'things were really happening'.

Addressing resolution issues

In the final stages of counselling Sue dealt with several resolution issues, the search for meaning being the most predominant. At this point, she claimed that she no longer hated her father – although she did hate what he had done to her, her mother, and her siblings. Sue also reported that she no longer wished her father harm, as she once had. However, she expressed a strong need to know 'why he did what he did'. Her attempt to understand the cause of the abuse became the focus of several counselling sessions. In the following interaction, Sue begins to seek an answer to this question and the counsellor encourages her search:

> *Sue*: I just cannot understand why anyone would do that to his little girls. Was he sick or was he evil? He'll have to pay in hell, one way or the other. Maybe it was the alcohol. I guess it really doesn't matter, it happened.
>
> *Counsellor*: I know I've heard you wonder before why your father did what he did, so perhaps it is an important question for you. There may not be a definite answer – and whatever the answer, the abuse was wrong. However, many individuals who have had a traumatic experience wonder why it happened.
>
> *Sue*: I do wonder a lot. I think about him a lot now. I know he was an alcoholic, but there are many alcoholics who don't abuse their children. I've read that sometimes those who abuse their children were abused themselves. I suspect that might be true of my father. I do know my grandfather was in jail for a long stretch; I think it was for assaulting someone in a bar. Maybe even for killing someone. So he could not have been a model parent. My grandmother, she was weird. She was a cold fish.
>
> *Counsellor*: So you would guess that your father had some pretty poor parenting himself.
>
> *Sue*: I'm sure he did. I suspect he was beaten, probably a lot.
>
> *Counsellor*: That might be a possibility. Sometimes, those who abuse others were abused themselves.
>
> *Sue*: You know I wouldn't be surprised if my mother was also abused. Both her parents died of alcoholism – you know, liver problems – so at the very least she probably had a miserable childhood. Us kids probably didn't stand a chance of getting good parents.

Sue also found meaning in her experience by coming to believe that some benefit had come from her healing process. In the following interaction, she comes to this conclusion:

Sue: Now that I'm doing so well, someone in AA asked me the other day if I'm glad the abuse happened because it made me tough.
Counsellor: What did you say?
Sue: No, I'm not glad. That's silly. This has been too painful and I lost too many good years of my life because of it. But, as bad as it was to be abused and to be a hermit for all those years, something good has come from this. Paula and I are close in a way we have never been before. Did you know I'm going to see her over my vacation? Also, now I know I'm strong. Everyone told me this, but now I believe it.

Relinquishing the survivor identity was also a significant step for Sue, as reflected in the following interaction with the counsellor:

Sue: It's funny, for most of my life I never thought of myself as an incest victim. Then, for a year, it was all I could think about. I was obsessed with it. Now, things are good. I have other things to think about. I'll never forget it [the abuse], of course, but it doesn't rule my life.
Counsellor: Yes, your abuse is an important part of your history. Due to your strength and all the work you've put into dealing with it, however, it no longer guides your life. You've moved beyond thinking of yourself primarily as an incest survivor.

Shortly after this interaction, Sue decided to end counselling. She spent several more sessions reviewing her progress, stating future goals, and saying goodbye to the counsellor. She said she believed that she would continue to expand her circle of friends and was contemplating beginning college. She visited her mother periodically, but was no longer her caretaker. Although she was sad and a bit scared to be ending counselling, Sue believed she had made significant progress and stated that she now felt healthy.

Discussion

The counselling interventions used at this stage validated Sue's need to search for meaning. Because Sue's search involved deciding why her father had abused her, exploring possible causes of his abusive behavior (e.g. his own childhood abuse) enhanced the resolution process. The counsellor also facilitated discussion of two other resolution issues for Sue: finding benefit from her healing experience (e.g. her strength, her close relationship with Paula) and giving up the survivor role.

References

Adams-Wescott, J. and Isenbart, D. (1996) 'Creating preferred relationships: the politics of recovery from child sexual abuse', *Journal of Systemic Therapies*, 15 (1): 13–30.

Agosta, C. and Loring, M. (1988) 'Understanding and treating the adult retrospective victim of child sexual abuse', in S. M. Sgroi (ed.), *Vulnerable populations: Vol. 1. Evaluation and treatment of sexually abused children and adult survivors.* Lexington, MA: Lexington Books. pp. 115–36.

Allen, C. V. (1980) *Daddy's girl.* New York: Berkeley Books.

Angelou, M. (1971) *I know why the caged bird sings.* New York: Bantam Books.

Armstrong, L. (1978) *Kiss daddy goodnight.* New York: Pocket Books.

Bass, E. and Davis, L. (1994) *The courage to heal: a guide for women survivors of child abuse,* (3rd edn). New York: HarperPerennial.

Bass, E. and Thornton, L. (eds) (1983) *I never told anyone: writings by women survivors of child sexual abuse.* New York: Harper and Row.

Beck, A. (1994) 'Workshop on cognitive therapy of personality disorders'. Evolution of Psychotherapy Conference, Hamburg, Germany.

Becker, J. V., Skinner, L. J., Abel, G. G. and Cichon, J. (1986) 'Level of postassault sexual functioning in rape and incest victims', *Archives of Sexual Behavior*, 15 (1): 37–49.

Beitchman, J. H., Zucker, K. J., Hood, J. E., daCosta, G. A., Akman, D. and Cassavia, E. (1992) 'A review of the long-term effects of child sexual abuse', *Child Abuse & Neglect*, 16: 101–17.

Bernstein, D. P., Fink, L., Handelsman, L., Foote, J., Lovejoy, M., Wenzel, K., Sapareta, E. and Ruggiero, J. (1994) 'Initial reliability and validity of a new retrospective measure of child abuse and neglect', *American Journal of Psychiatry*, 151 (8): 1132–6.

Bernstein, E. M. and Putnam, F. W. (1986) 'Development, reliability, and validity of a dissociation scale', *Journal of Nervous and Mental Disease*, 174 (12): 727–35.

Bifulco, A., Brown, G. W. and Adler, Z. (1991) 'Early sexual abuse and clinical depression in adult life', *British Journal of Psychiatry*, 159: 115–22.

Blake-White, J. and Kline, C. M. (1985) 'Treating the dissociative process in adult victims of childhood incest', *Social Casework: The Journal of Contemporary Social Work*, 66: 394–402.

Bolton, F. G., Morris, L. A. and MacEachron, A. E. (1989) *Males at risk: the other side of child sexual abuse.* Newbury Park, CA: Sage.

Brady, K. (1979) *Father's days.* New York: Dell.

Braun, B. G. (1988) 'The BASK model of dissociation', *Dissociation: progress in the dissociative disorders*, 1 (1): 4–23.

Briere, J. (1989) *Therapy for adults molested as children*. New York: Springer.

Briere, J. (1992) *Child abuse trauma: theory and treatment of lasting effects*. Newbury Park, CA: Sage.

Briere, J. (1995) *Trauma Symptom Inventory: professional manual*. Odessa, FL: Psychological Assessment Resources.

Briere, J. (1996) 'A self-trauma model for treating adult survivors of severe child abuse', in J. Briere, L. Berliner, J. A. Bulkely, C. Jeeny and T. Reid (eds), *The APSAC handbook on child maltreatment*. Thousand Oaks, CA: Sage. pp. 140–57.

Briere, J. (1997) 'Assessment of child abuse effects in adults', in J. P. Wilson and T. M. Keane (eds), *Assessing psychological trauma and PTSD*. New York: Guilford Press. pp. 43–68.

Briere, J. and Conte, J. (1993) 'Self-reported amnesia for abuse in adults molested as children', *Journal of Traumatic Stress*, 6 (1): 21–31.

Briere, J. and Elliot, D. M. (1993) 'Sexual abuse, family environment and psychological symptoms: on the validity of statistical control', *Journal of Consulting and Clinical Psychology*, 61: 284–8.

Briere, J. and Runtz, M. (1988) 'Post sexual abuse trauma', in G. E. Wyatt and G. J. Powell (eds), *Lasting effects of child sexual abuse*. Newbury Park, CA: Sage. pp. 85–99.

Briere, J. and Runtz, M. (1989) 'The Trauma Symptom Checklist (TSC-33): early data on a new scale', *Journal of Interpersonal Violence*, 4 (2): 151–63.

Briere, J. and Runtz, M. (1990) 'Differential adult symptomatology associated with three types of child abuse histories', *Child Abuse and Neglect*, 14: 357–64.

Brower, K. J., Blow, F. C. and Beresford, T. P. (1989) 'Treatment implications of chemical dependency models: an integrative approach', *Journal of Substance Abuse Treatment*, 6 (3): 147–57.

Brown, D., Scheflin, A. W. and Hammond, D. C. (1998) *Memory, trauma treatment, and the law: an essential reference on memory for clinicians, researchers, attorneys, and judges*. New York: W. W. Norton.

Brown, D. P. and Fromm, E. (1986) *Hypnotherapy and hypnoanalysis*. Hillsdale, NJ: L. Erlbaum and Associates.

Browne, A. and Finkelhor, D. (1986) 'Impact of child sexual abuse: a review of the research', *Psychological Bulletin*, 99: 66–77.

Bruckner, D. F. and Johnson, P. E. (1987) 'Treatment for adult male victims of childhood sexual abuse', *Social Casework: The Journal of Contemporary Social Work*, 68: 81–7.

Bushnell, J. A., Wells, J. E. and Oakley-Browne, M. A. (1992) 'Long-term effects of intra-familial sexual abuse in childhood', *Acta Psychiatrica Scandinavica*, 85 (2): 136–42.

Calam, R. and Slade, P. D. (1987) 'Eating problems and sexual experience: some relationships', *British Review of Bulimia Anorexia*, 2 (1): 37–43.

Calam, R. M. and Slade, P. D. (1989) 'Sexual experience and eating problems in female undergraduates', *International Journal of Eating Disorders*, 8 (4): 391–7.

Cameron, C. (1994) 'Women survivors confronting their abusers: issues, decisions and outcomes', *Journal of Child Sexual Abuse*, 3 (1): 7–35.

Carlson, S. (1990) 'The victim/perpetrator: turning points in therapy', in M. Hunter (ed.), *The sexually abused male: Vol. 2. Application of treatment strategies*. Lexington, MA: Lexington Books. pp. 249–66.

Carson, D. K., Gertz, L. M., Donaldson, M. A. and Wonderlich, S. A. (1990)

'Family-of-origin characteristics and current family relationships of female adult incest victims', *Journal of Family Violence*, 5 (2): 153–71.

Ceci, S. J. and Bruck, M. (1993) 'Suggestibility of the child witness: a historical review and synthesis', *Psychological Bulletin*, 113 (3): 403–39.

Ceci, S. J., Huffman, M. L. C., Smith, E. and Loftus, E. F. (1994) 'Repeatedly thinking about a non-event: source misattributions among preschoolers', *Consciousness & cognition*, 3: 388–407.

Chu, J. A. (1998) *Rebuilding shattered lives*. New York: John Wiley & Sons.

Chu, J. A. and Dill, D. L. (1990) 'Dissociative symptoms in relation to childhood physical and sexual abuse', *American Journal of Psychiatry*, 147 (7): 887–92.

Cloitre, M. (1998) 'Sexual revictimization: risk factors and prevention', in V. M. Follette, J. I. Ruzek and F. R. Abueg (eds), *Cognitive behavioral therapies for trauma*. New York: Guilford Press. pp. 278–304.

Cole, C. H. and Barney, E. E. (1987) 'Safeguards and the therapeutic window: a group treatment strategy for adult incest survivors', *American Journal of Orthopsychiatry*, 57: 601–9.

Cole, C. L. (1985) 'A group design for adult female survivors of childhood incest', *Women and Therapy*, 4 (3): 71–82.

Conte, J. (1999) 'Memory, research, and the law: future directions', in L. M. Williams and V. L. Banyard (eds), *Trauma and memory*. Thousand Oaks, CA: Sage. pp. 77–92.

Courtois, C. A. (1999) *Recollections of sexual abuse: treatment principles and guidelines*. New York: W. W. Norton.

Cunningham, R. M., Stiffman, A. R., Dore, P. and Earls, F. (1994) 'The association of physical and sexual abuse with HIV risk behaviors in adolescence and young adulthood: implications for public health', *Child Abuse and Neglect*, 18 (3): 233–45.

Daugherty, L. B. (1984) *Why me?* Racine, WI: Mother Courage Press.

Davis, L. (1990) *The courage to heal workbook*. New York: Harper and Row.

Demaré, D. (1993) 'The childhood maltreatment questionnaire'. Unpublished manuscript. University of Manitoba, Winnipeg, Canada.

Draucker, C. B and Petrovic, K. (1996) 'The healing of adult male survivors of childhood sexual abuse', *Image: Journal of Nursing Scholarship*, 28 (4): 325–30.

Draucker, C. B and Petrovic, K. (1997) 'Therapy with male survivors of sexual abuse: the client perspective', *Issues in Mental Health Nursing*, 18: 139–55.

Draucker, C. B. (1989) 'Cognitive adaptation of female incest survivors', *Journal of Consulting and Clinical Psychology*, 57: 668–70.

Draucker, C. B. (1992a) 'Construing benefit from a negative experience of incest', *Western Journal of Nursing Research*, 14 (3): 343–57.

Draucker, C. B. (1992b) 'The healing process of female adult survivors: constructing a personal residence', *Image: Journal of Nursing Scholarship*, 24 (1): 4–8.

Draucker, C. B. (1993) 'Childhood sexual abuse: sources of trauma', *Issues in Mental Health Nursing*, 14: 249–62.

Draucker, C. B. (1995) 'A coping model: adult survivors of childhood sexual abuse', *Journal of Interpersonal Violence*, 10 (2): 159–75.

Draucker, C. B. (1996) 'Family-of-origin variables and adult female survivors of childhood sexual abuse: a review of the research', *Journal of Child Sexual Abuse*, 5 (4): 35–63.

Draucker, C. B. (1997) 'Early family life and victimization in the lives of women', *Research in Nursing and Health*, 20: 399–412.

Draucker, C. B. (1998) 'Narrative therapy for women who have lived with violence', *Archives of Psychiatric Nursing*, 12 (3): 162–8.

Drossman, D. A., Leserman, J., Nachman, G., Li, Z., Gluck, H., Toomey, T. C. and Mitchell, C. M. (1990) 'Sexual and physical abuse in women with functional or organic gastrointestinal disorders', *Annuals of Internal Medicine*, 113: 828–33.

Edwards, J. J. and Alexander, P. C. (1992) 'The contribution of family background to the long-term adjustment of women sexually abused as children', *Journal of Interpersonal Violence*, 7 (3): 306–20.

Elliott, D. M. (1992) 'Traumatic events survey'. Unpublished psychological test, Harbor-UCLA Medical Center, Los Angeles.

Elliott, D. M. and Briere, J. (1992) 'Sexual abuse trauma among professional women: validating the Trauma Symptom Checklist-40 (TSC-40)', *Child Abuse and Neglect*, 16: 391–8.

Elliott, D. M. and Briere, J. (1993) 'Childhood maltreatment, later revictimization, and adult symptomatology: a causal analysis'. Paper presented at the 101st Annual Meeting of the American Psychological Association, Toronto, Canada, August.

Elliott, D. M. and Briere, J. (1995) 'Post-traumatic stress associated with delayed recall of sexual abuse: a general population study', *Journal of Traumatic Stress*, 8: 629–47.

Erikson, E. (1968) *Identity: youth and crisis*. New York: Norton.

Evans, M. C. (1990) 'Brother to brother: integrating concepts of healing regarding male sexual assault survivors and Vietnam veterans', in M. Hunter (ed.), *The sexually abused male: Vol. 2. Application of treatment strategies*. Lexington, MA: Lexington Books. pp. 57–78.

Faria, G. and Belohlavek, N. (1984) 'Treating female adult survivors of incest', *Social Casework*, 65: 465–71.

Farmer, S. (1989) *Adult children of abusive parents*. Chicago: Contemporary Books.

Felitti, V. J. (1991) 'Long-term medical consequences of incest, rape, and molestation', *Southern Medical Journal*, 84 (3): 328–31.

Finkelhor, D. (1990) 'Early and long-term effects of child sexual abuse: an update', *Professional Psychology: Research and Practice*, 21 (5): 325–30.

Finkelhor, D. (1993) 'Epidemiological factors in the clinical identification of child sexual abuse', *Child Abuse and Neglect*, 17: 67–70.

Finkelhor, D. (1994) 'The international epidemiology of child sexual abuse', *Child Abuse and Neglect*, 18 (5): 409–17.

Finkelhor, D. (1997) 'Child sexual abuse', in O. W. Barnett, C. L. Miller-Perrin and R. D. Perrin (eds), *Family violence across the lifespan*. Thousand Oaks, CA: Sage. pp. 69–104.

Finkelhor, D. and Russell, D. (1984) 'Women as perpetrators: review of the evidence', in D. Finkelhor (ed.), *Child sexual abuse: new theory and research*. New York: Free Press. pp. 171–87.

Finkelhor, D., Hotaling, G. T., Lewis, I. A. and Smith, C. (1990) 'Sexual abuse in a national survey of adult men and women: prevalence, characteristics, and risk factors', *Child Abuse and Neglect*, 14: 19–28.

Foy, D. W., Sipprelle, R. C., Rueger, D. B. and Carroll, E. M. (1984) 'Etiology of post-traumatic stress syndrome in Vietnam veterans: analysis of premilitary,

military, and combat exposure influences', *Journal of Consulting and Clinical Psychology*, 52 (1): 79–87.

Freedman, J. and Combs, G. (1996) *Narrative therapy: the social construction of preferred realities*. New York: W. W. Norton.

Friedman, M. A. and Brownell, K. D. (1996) *A comprehensive treatment manual for the management of obesity*. New York: Plenum Press.

Friedman, M. J. and Schnurr, P. P. (1995) 'The relationship between trauma, posttraumatic stress disorder, and physical health', in M. J. Friedman, D. S. Charney and A. Y. Deutch (eds), *Neurobiological and clinical consequences of stress: from normal adaptation to PTSD*. Philadelphia: Lippincott-Raven. pp. 507–24.

Fromuth, M. E. and Burkhart, B. R. (1989) 'Long-term psychological correlates of childhood sexual abuse in two samples of college men', *Child Abuse and Neglect*, 13 (4): 533–42.

Fry, R. (1993) 'Adult physical illness and childhood sexual abuse', *Journal of Psychosomatic Research*, 37 (2): 89–103.

Garbarino, J., Guttman, E. and Seeley, J. W. (1986) *The psychologically battered child: strategies for identification, assessment and intervention*. San Francisco: Jossey-Bass.

Garner, D. M. and Garfinkel, P. E. (1997) *Handbook of psychotherapy for anorexia and bulimia*, 2nd edn. New York: Guilford Press.

Gelinas, D. J. (1983) 'The persisting negative effects of incest', *Psychiatry*, 46: 312–32.

Gerber, P. N. (1990) 'Victims becoming offenders: a study of ambiguities', in M. Hunter (ed.), *The sexually abused male: Vol. 1. Prevalence, impact, and treatment*. Lexington, MA: Lexington Books. pp. 153–76.

Gil, E. (1990) *Treatment of adult survivors of childhood sexual abuse*. Walnut Creek, CA: Launch.

Gold, E. R. (1986) 'Long-term effects of sexual victimization in childhood: an attributional approach', *Journal of Consulting and Clinical Psychology*, 54: 471–5.

Gold, S. N. and Brown, L. S. (1997) 'Therapeutic responses to delayed recall: beyond recovered memory', *Psychotherapy*, 34 (2): 182–91.

Gold, S. N., Hughes, D. and Hohnecker, L. (1994) 'Degrees of repression of sexual abuse memories', *American Psychologist*, 49 (5): 441–2.

Golding, J. M. (1994) 'Sexual assault history and physical health in randomly selected Los Angeles women', *Health Psychology*, 13 (2): 130–8.

Goodman, B. and Nowak-Scibelli, D. (1985) 'Group treatment for women incestuously abused as children', *International Journal of Group Psychotherapy*, 35: 531–44.

Gordon, M. and Alexander, P. C. (1993) 'Introduction of special issue: research on treatment of adults sexually abused in childhood', *Journal of Interpersonal Violence*, 8 (3): 307–11.

Gordy, P. L. (1983) 'Group work that supports adult victims of childhood incest', *Social Casework: The Journal of Contemporary Social Work*, 64: 300–7.

Gorski, T. (1992) *Understanding the twelve steps*. New York: Simon & Schuster.

Greenwald, E., Leitenberg, H., Cado, S. and Tarran, M. J. (1990) 'Childhood sexual abuse: long-term effects on psychological and sexual functioning in a nonclinical and nonstudent sample of adult women', *Child Abuse and Neglect*, 14: 503–13.

Gudjonsson, G. H. (1984) 'A new scale of interrogative suggestibility', *Personality and Individual Differences*, 5 (3): 303–14.

Hall, L. and Lloyd, S. (1989) *Surviving child sexual abuse*. New York: Falmer Press.

Hall, L. A., Sachs, B., Rayens, M. K. and Lutenbacher, M. (1993) 'Childhood physical and sexual abuse: their relationship with depressive symptoms in adulthood', *Image: Journal of Nursing Scholarship*, 25 (4): 317–23.

Hanson, R. K. (1990) 'The psychological impact of sexual assault on women and children: a review', *Annals of Sex Research*, 3: 187–232.

Harris, M. (1998) *Trauma recovery and empowerment: a clinician's guide for working with women in groups*. New York: The Free Press.

Harrop-Griffiths, J., Katon, W., Walker, E., Holm, L., Russo, J. and Hickok, L. (1988) 'The association between chronic pelvic pain, psychiatric diagnoses and childhood sexual abuse', *Obstetrics & Gynecology*, 71: 589–94.

Harvey, M. R. (1999) 'Memory research and clinical practice: a critique of three paradigms and a framework of psychotherapy with trauma survivors', in L. M. Williams and V. L. Banyard (eds), *Trauma and memory*. Thousand Oaks, CA: Sage. pp. 19–29.

Hathaway, S. R. and McKinley, J. C. (1967) *The Minnesota Multiphasic Personality Inventory Manual*. New York: Psychological Corporation.

Herman, J. L. (1981) *Father–daughter incest*. Cambridge, MA: Harvard University Press.

Herman, J. L. (1992) *Trauma and recovery*. New York: Basic Books.

Herman, J. L. and Schatzow, E. (1984) 'Time-limited group therapy for women with a history of incest', *International Journal of Group Psychotherapy*, 34: 605–15.

Herman, J. L. and Schatzow, E. (1987) 'Recovery and verification of memories of childhood sexual trauma', *Psychoanalytic Psychology*, 4: 1–14.

Holmes, D. S. (1990) 'The evidence for repression: an examination of sixty years of research', in J. L. Singer (ed.), *Repression and dissociation: implications for personality theory, psychopathology, and health*. Chicago: University of Chicago Press. pp. 85–102.

Horowitz, M. J. (1976) *Stress response syndromes*. New York: Jason Aronson.

Horowitz, M. J., Wilner, N. and Alvarez, W. (1979) 'Impacts of Event Scale: a measure of subjective stress', *Psychosocial Medicine*, 41 (3): 209–18.

Hunter, M. (1995) *Adult survivors of sexual abuse: treatment innovations*. Thousand Oaks, CA: Sage.

Hunter, M. and Gerber, P. N. (1990) 'Use of terms victim and survivor in the grief stages commonly seen during recovery from sexual abuse', in M. Hunter (ed.), *The sexually abused male: Vol. 2. Application of treatment strategies*. Lexington, MA: Lexington Books. pp. 79–89.

Hyman, I. E., Husband, T. H. and Billings, F. J. (1995) 'False memories of childhood experiences', *Applied Cognitive Psychology*, 9 (3): 181–97.

Hyman, I. E. and Pentland, J. (1996) 'The role of mental imagery and the creation of false childhood memories', *Journal of Memory and Language*, 35 (2): 101–17.

Jackson, J. L., Calhoun, K. S., Amick, A. E., Maddever, H. M. and Habif, V. L. (1990) 'Young adult women who report childhood intrafamiliar sexual abuse: subsequent adjustment', *Archives of Sexual Behavior*, 19 (3): 211–21.

Janet, P. (1925/1976) *Psychological healing*. New York: Macmillan.

Janoff-Bulman, R. (1992) *Shattered assumptions: towards a new psychology of trauma*. New York: The Free Press.

Jehu, D. (1990) *Beyond sexual abuse: therapy with women who were childhood victims*. New York: Wiley.

Jehu, D., Gazan, M. and Klassen, C. (1988) *Beyond sexual abuse: therapy with women who were childhood victims*. Chichester, UK: John Wiley & Sons.

Jehu, D., Klassen, C. and Gazan, M. (1986) 'Cognitive restructuring of distorted beliefs associated with childhood sexual abuse', *Journal of Social Work and Human Sexuality*, 4: 49–69.

Johanek, M. F. (1988) 'Treatment of male victims of child sexual abuse in military service', in S. M. Sgroi (ed.), *Vulnerable populations: Vol. 1. Evaluation and treatment of sexually abused children and adult survivors*. Lexington, MA: Lexington Books. pp. 103–14.

Josephson, G. S. and Fong-Beyette, M. L. (1987) 'Factors assisting female clients' disclosure of incest during counseling', *Journal of Counseling and Development*, 65: 475–8.

Joy, S. (1987) 'Retrospective presentations of incest: treatment strategies for use with adult women', *Journal of Counseling and Development*, 65: 317–19.

Kasl, C. D. (1990) 'Female perpetrators of sexual abuse: a feminist view', in M. Hunter (ed.), *The sexually abused male: Vol. 1. Prevalence, impact, and treatment*. Lexington, MA: Lexington Books. pp. 259–74.

Kinsey, A. C., Pomeroy, W. B., Martin, C. E. and Gebhard, P. H. (1953) *Sexual behavior in the human female*. Philadelpha: Saunders.

Kluft, R. P. (1996) 'Treating the traumatic memories of patients with dissociative identity disorder', *American Journal of Psychiatry*, 153 (Suppl.): 103–10.

Landis, J. (1956) 'Experiences of 500 children with adult sexual deviances', *Psychiatric Quarterly Supplement*, 30: 91–109.

Laws, A. (1993) 'Does a history of sexual abuse in childhood play a role in women's medical problems? A review', *Journal of Women's Health*, 2 (2): 165–72.

Lepine, D. (1990) 'Ending the cycle of violence: overcoming guilt in incest survivors', in T. A. Laidlaw and C. Malmo (eds), *Healing voices*. San Francisco: Jossey-Bass. pp. 272–87.

Lindsay, D. S. (1990) 'Misleading suggestions can impair eyewitnesses' ability to remember event details', *Journal of Experimental Psychology: Learning, Memory and Cognition*, 16 (6): 1077–83.

Lindsay, D. S. (1994) 'Memory source monitoring and eyewitness testimony', in D. F. Ross, J. D. Read and M. P. Toglia (eds), *Adult eye witness testimony: current trends and developments*. New York: Cambridge University Press. pp. 27–55.

Lindsay, D. S. and Read, J. D. (1994) 'Psychotherapy and memories of childhood sexual abuse: a cognitive perspective', *Applied Cognitive Psychology*, 8: 281–338.

Linehan, M. M. (1993) *Cognitive-behavioral treatment of borderline personality disorder*. New York: Guilford Press.

Loftus, E. F. (1993) 'The reality of repressed memories', *American Psychologist*, 48 (5): 518–37.

Loftus, E. F. and Picrell, J. E. (1995) 'The formation of false memories', *Psychiatric Annals*, 25: 720–5.

Madden, R. G. (1998) *Legal issues in social work, counseling, and mental health*. Thousand Oaks, CA: Sage.

Maltz, W. and Holman, B. (1987) *Incest and sexuality*. Lexington, MA: Lexington Books.

Masters, W. H. and Johnson, V. E. (1970) *Human sexual inadequacy*. Boston: Little, Brown.

Matthews, R., Matthews, J. and Speltz, K. (1990) 'Female sexual offenders', in M. Hunter (ed.), *The sexually abused male: Vol. 1. Prevalence, impact, and treatment*. Lexington, MA: Lexington Books. pp. 275–94.

McCarthy, B. W. (1990) 'Treating sexual dysfunction associated with prior sexual trauma', *Journal of Sex and Marital Therapy*, 16 (3): 142–6.

McCauley, J., Kern, D. E., Kolodner, K., Dill, L., Schroeder, A. F., DeChant, H. K., Ryden, J., Derogatis, L. R. and Bass, E. B. (1997) 'Clinical characteristics of women with a history of childhood abuse: unhealed wounds', *JAMA*, 277 (17): 1362–8.

McNaron, T. and Morgan, Y. (eds) (1982) *Voices in the night: women speaking about incest.* Minneapolis: Cleis Press.

Meichenbaum, D. (1994) *A clinical handbook/practical therapist manual.* Ontario, Canada: Institute Press.

Millon, T. (1994) *Manual for the MCMI-III.* Minneapolis: National Computer Systems.

Moeller, T. P., Bachman, G. A. and Moeller, J. R. (1993) 'The combined effects of physical, sexual and emotional abuse during childhood: long-term health consequences for women', *Child Abuse and Neglect*, 17 (5): 623–40.

Nash, M. R., Hulsey, T. L., Sexton, M. C., Harralson, T. L. and Lambert, W. (1993) 'Long-term sequelae of childhood sexual abuse: perceived family environment, psychopathology, and dissociation', *Journal of Consulting and Clinical Psychology*, 61 (2): 276–83.

National Center on Child Abuse and Neglect (1978) *Child sexual abuse: incest, assault, and sexual exploitation, a special report.* Washington, DC: NCCAN.

O'Toole, A. W. and Welt, S. R. (1989) *Interpersonal theory in nursing practice: selected works of Hildegard E. Peplau.* New York: Springer.

Parker, S. and Parker, H. (1991) 'Female victims of child sexual abuse: adult adjustment', *Journal of Family Violence*, 6 (2): 183–97.

Pecukonis, E. V. (1996) 'Childhood sexual abuse in women with chronic intractable back pain', *Social Work in Health Care*, 23 (3): 1–16.

Polusny, M. A. and Follette, V. M. (1995) 'Long-term correlates of child sexual abuse: theory and review of the empirical literature', *Applied & Preventive Psychology*, 4: 143–66.

Pribor, E. F. and Dinwiddie, S. H. (1992) 'Psychiatric correlates of incest in childhood', *American Journal of Psychiatry*, 149 (1): 52–6.

Ramsey, J. (1979) 'Dealing with the last taboo', *Siecus Report*, 7: 1–2, 6–7.

Rausch, K. and Knutson, J. F. (1991) 'The self-report of personal punitive childhood experiences and those of siblings', *Child Abuse and Neglect*, 15 (1–2): 29–36.

Reiter, R. C. and Gambone, J. C. (1990) 'Demographic and historic variables in women with idiopathic chronic pelvic pain', *Obstetrics & Gynecology*, 75 (3, Pt. 1): 428–32.

Reiter, R. C., Shakerin, L. R., Gambone, J. C. and Milburn, A. K. (1991) 'Correlation between sexual abuse and somatization in women with somatic and nonsomatic chronic pain', *American Journal of Obstetrics and Gynecology*, 165 (1): 104–9.

Roland, B. C., Zelhart, P. and Dubes, R. (1989) 'MMPI correlates of college women who reported experiencing child/adult sexual contact with father, stepfather, or with other persons', *Psychological Reports*, 64 (3, Pt. 2): 1159–62.

Satir, V. (1988) *The new peoplemaking.* Mountain View, CA: Science and Behavior Books.

Saunders, B. E., Villeponteaux, L. A., Lipovsky, J. A., Kilpatrick, D. G. and Veronen, L. J. (1992) 'Child sexual assault as a risk factor for mental disorders among women: a community survey', *Journal of Interpersonal Violence*, 7 (2): 189–204.

Schwartz, M. F. and Masters, W. H. (1993) 'Integration of trauma-based, cognitive behavioral, systemic and addiction approaches for treatment of hypersexual pair-bonding', *Sexual Addiction and Compulsivity*, 1: 57–76.

Sepler, F. (1990) 'Victim advocacy and young male victims of sexual abuse: an evolutionary model', in M. Hunter (ed.), *The sexually abused male: Vol. 1. Prevalence, impact, and treatment*. Lexington, MA: Lexington Books. pp. 73–86.

Sgroi, S. M. (1989a) 'Stages of recovery for adult survivors', in S. M. Sgroi (ed.), *Vulnerable populations: Vol. 2. Sexual abuse treatment for children, adult survivors, and persons with mental retardation*. Lexington, MA: Lexington Books. pp. 111–30.

Sgroi, S. M. (1989b) 'Healing together: peer group therapy for adult survivors of child sexual abuse', in S. M. Sgroi (ed.), *Vulnerable populations: Vol. 2. Sexual abuse treatment for children, adult survivors, and persons with mental retardation*. Lexington, MA: Lexington Books. pp. 131–66.

Sgroi, S. M. and Bunk, B. S. (1988) 'A clinical approach to adult survivors of child sexual abuse', in S. M. Sgroi (ed.), *Vulnerable populations: Vol. 1. Evaluation and treatment of sexually abused children and adult survivors*. Lexington, MA: Lexington Books. pp. 137–86.

Silver, R. L., Boon, C. and Stones, M. H. (1983) 'Searching for meaning in misfortune: making sense of incest', *Journal of Social Issues*, 39 (2): 81–102.

Sisk, S. L. and Hoffman, C. F. (1987) *Inside scars*. Gainesville, FL: Pandora Press.

Skorina, J. K. and Kovach, J. A. (1986) 'Treatment techniques for incest-related issues in alcoholic women', *Alcoholism Treatment Quarterly*, 3 (1): 17–30.

Smolak, L., Levine, M. P. and Sullins, E. (1990) 'Are child sexual experiences related to eating-disordered attitudes and behaviors in a college sample?', *International Journal of Eating Disorders*, 9: 167–78.

Spiegel, D. and Spiegel, H. (1987) 'Forensic uses of hypnosis', in I. B. Weiner and A. K. Hess (eds), *Handbook of forensic psychology*. New York: Wiley. pp. 490–507.

Springs, F. E. and Friedrich, W. N. (1992) 'Health risk behaviors and medical sequelae of childhood sexual abuse', *Mayo Clinic Proceedings*, 67: 527–32.

Stein, J. A., Golding, J. M., Siegel, J. M., Burnam, M. A. and Sorenson, S. B. (1988) 'Long-term psychological sequelae of child sexual abuse: the Los Angeles Epidemiologic Catchment Area Study', in G. E. Wyatt and G. J. Powell (eds), *Lasting effects of child sexual abuse*. Newbury Park, CA: Sage. pp. 135–54.

Struve, J. (1990) 'Dancing with the patriarchy: the politics of sexual abuse', in M. Hunter (ed.), *The sexually abused male: Vol. 1. Prevalence, impact, and treatment*. Lexington, MA: Lexington Books. pp. 3–46.

Swanson, L. and Biaggio, M. K. (1985) 'Therapeutic perspectives on father–daughter incest', *The American Journal of Psychiatry*, 142: 667–74.

Taylor, S. E. (1983) 'Adjustment to threatening events: a theory of cognitive adaptation', *American Psychologist*, 38: 1161–73.

Thomas, T. (1989) *Men surviving incest*. Walnut Creek, CA: Launch.

Trotter, C. (1995) 'Stages of recovery and relapse prevention for the chemically dependent adult sexual trauma survivor', in M. Hunter (ed.), *Adult survivors of sexual abuse: treatment innovations*. Thousand Oaks, CA: Sage. pp. 98–135.

Tsai, M. and Wagner, N. N. (1978) 'Therapy groups for women sexually molested as children', *Archives of Sexual Behavior*, 7: 417–27.

Urquiza, A. J. and Capra, M. (1990) 'The impact of sexual abuse: initial and long-term effects', in M. Hunter (ed.), *The sexually abused male: Vol. 1. Prevalence, impact, and treatment*. Lexington, MA: Lexington Books. pp. 105–36.

Urquiza, A. J. and Keating, L. M. (1990) 'The prevalence of the sexual victimization of males', in M. Hunter (ed.), *The sexually abused male: Vol. 1. Prevalence, impact, and treatment*. Lexington, MA: Lexington Books. pp. 89–104.

US Department of Health and Human Services, Administration for Children and Families, National Center on Child Abuse and Neglect (1996) *The third national incidence study of child abuse and neglect (1993)*. Washington, DC: Author.

Van der Kolk, B. A. and van der Hart, O. (1991) 'The intrusive past: the flexibility of memory and the engraving of trauma', *American Imago*, 48 (4): 425–54.

Waigandt, A., Wallace, D. L., Phelps, L. and Miller, D. A. (1990) 'The impact of sexual assault on physical health status', *Journal of Traumatic Stress*, 3 (1): 93–102.

Walker, E., Katon, W., Harrop-Griffiths, J., Holm, L., Russo, J. and Hickok, L. R. (1988) 'Relationship of chronic pelvic pain to psychiatric diagnoses and childhood sexual abuse', *American Journal of Psychiatry*, 145 (1): 75–80.

Walker, E. A., Katon, W. J., Hanson, J., Harrop-Griffiths, J., Holm, L., Jones, M. L., Hickok, L. and Jemelka, R. P. (1993) 'Medical and psychiatric symptoms in women with childhood sexual abuse', *Psychosomatic Medicine*, 54: 658–64.

Walker, E. A., Katon, W. J., Neraas, K., Jemelka, R. P. and Massoth, D. (1992) 'Dissociation in women with chronic pelvic pain', *American Journal of Psychiatry*, 149 (4): 534–7.

Waller, G. (1991) 'Sexual abuse as a factor in eating disorders', *British Journal of Psychiatry*, 159: 664–71.

Waller, G. (1992a) 'Sexual abuse and bulimic symptoms in eating disorders: do family interaction and self-esteem explain the links?', *International Journal of Eating Disorders*, 12 (3): 235–40.

Waller, G. (1992b) 'Sexual abuse and the severity of bulimic symptoms', *British Journal of Psychiatry*, 161: 90–3.

Webb, L. P. and Leehan, J. (1996) *Group treatment for adult survivors of abuse*. Thousand Oaks, CA: Sage.

Wegscheider-Cruse, S. (1985) *Choicemaking*. Deerfield Beach, FL: Health Communications.

Weingardt, K. R., Toland, H. K. and Loftus, E. F. (1994) 'Reports of suggested memories: do people truly believe them?', in D. F. Ross, J. D. Read and M. P. Toglia (eds), *Adult eyewitness testimony: current trends and developments*. New York: Cambridge University Press. pp. 3–26.

Westerlund, E. (1983) 'Counseling women with histories of incest', *Women and Therapy*, 2 (4): 17–31.

Westerlund, E. (1992) *Women's sexuality after childhood incest*. New York: W. W. Norton.

White, M. (1989) *Selected papers*. Adelaide, Australia: Dulwich Centre Publications.

White, M. (1992) *Experience, contradiction, narrative, and imagination*. Adelaide, Australia: Dulwich Centre Publications.

White, M. (1995) *Re-authoring lives: interviews and essays*. Adelaide, Australia: Dulwich Centre Publications.

White, M. and Epston, D. (1990) *Narrative means to therapeutic ends*. New York: W. W. Norton.

Whitfield, C. L. (1989) *Health the child within*. Deerfield Beach, FL: Health Communications.

Wiehe, V. R. (1990) *Sibling abuse*. Lexington, MA: Lexington Books.

Williams, L. M. (1994) 'Recall of childhood trauma: a prospective study of women's memories of child sexual abuse', *Journal of Counseling and Clinical Psychology*, 62 (2): 1167–76.

Wind, T. W. and Silvern, L. (1992) 'Type and extent of child abuse as predictors of adult functioning', *Journal of Family Violence*, 7 (4): 261–81.

Wurtele, S. K. and Miller-Perrin, C. L. (1992) *Preventing child sexual abuse: sharing the responsibility*. Lincoln: University of Nebraska Press.

Wyatt, G. E. and Newcomb, M. D. (1990) 'Internal and external mediators of women's sexual abuse in childhood', *Journal of Consulting and Clinical Psychology*, 58 (6): 758–67.

Wyatt, G. E., Guthrie, D. and Notgrass, C. M. (1992) 'Differential effects of women's child sexual abuse and subsequent revictimization', *Journal of Consulting and Clinical Psychology*, 60 (2): 167–73.

Yama, M. F., Tovey, S. L. and Fogas, B. S. (1993) 'Childhood family environment and sexual abuse as predicting of anxiety and depression in adult women', *American Journal of Orthopsychiatry*, 63 (1): 136–41.

Yama, M. F., Tovey, S. L., Fogas, B. S. and Teegarden, L. A. (1992) 'Joint consequences of parental alcoholism and childhood sexual abuse, and their partial mediation by family environment', *Violence and Victims*, 7 (4): 313–25.

Zierler, S., Feingold, L., Laufer, D., Velentgas, P., Kantrowtiz-Gordon, I. and Mayer, K. (1991) 'Adult survivors of childhood sexual abuse and subsequent risk for HIV infection', *American Journal of Public Health*, 81 (5): 572–5.

Index